Taunton's
BUILD LIKE A PRO™
EXPERT ADVICE FROM START TO FINISH

Built-ins

Taunton's

BUILD LIKE A PRO™
EXPERT ADVICE FROM START TO FINISH

Built-ins

Robert J. Settich

The Taunton Press

The Taunton Press
Inspiration for hands-on living®

The Taunton Press, Inc., 63 South Main Street, P.O. Box 5506, Newtown, CT 06470-5506

e-mail: tp@taunton.com

EDITOR: Martin Miller

COPY EDITOR: Seth Reichgott

INDEXER: Jay Kreider

JACKET/COVER DESIGN: Kimberly Adis

INTERIOR DESIGN: Kimberly Adis

LAYOUT: Cathy Cassidy

ILLUSTRATOR: Mario Ferro

PHOTOGRAPHER: Robert J. Settich, except where noted

Build Like a Pro™ is a trademark of The Taunton Press, Inc., registered in the U.S. Patent and Trademark Office.

Library of Congress Cataloging-in-Publication Data

Settich, Robert J.
  Built-ins / Robert Settich.
     p. cm.
  ISBN 978-1-56158-873-2
  1. Built-in furniture. 2. Cabinetwork. I. Title.
  TT197.5.B8S35 2009
  684.1'6--dc22

                                    2008013632

Printed in the United States of America
10 9 8 7 6 5 4 3 2 1

The following manufacturers/names appearing in *Built-ins* are trademarks: Accuride®, American Woodmark®, Blum®, Blumotion®, Bosch®, Closet Maid,® Confirmat®, Corian®, Festool®, Floetrol®, General Finishes®, Gibraltar®, Incra®, Jorgensen®, Lee Valley®, Leigh®, Masonite®, Medex®, Penetrol®, Rockler®, Space Balls®, Spax®, Titebond®, True Angle®, Tru-Grip®, Watco®

Working wood is inherently dangerous. Using hand or power tools improperly or ignoring safety practices can lead to permanent injury or even death. Don't try to perform operations you learn about here (or elsewhere) unless you're certain they are safe for you. If something about an operation doesn't feel right, don't do it. Look for another way. We want you to enjoy the craft, so please keep safety foremost in your mind whenever you're in the shop.

For my wife, Barbara, and our daughters Laura Greene and Diane Beers

ACKNOWLEDGMENTS

I extend my deep appreciation to the firms whose cooperation made this book possible. American Woodmark provided the cabinets shown in Chapter 11, as well as a design concept that maximized the space. Special thanks also to the firms who generously shared their in-depth product knowledge and technical advice. Several of these companies also furnished products for evaluation and photography. My appreciation to Leigh Industries (router jigs), Taylor Design Group (Incra Fence), Julius Blum® (hardware), Cut-N-Crown (crown molding jig), Festool®, Forrest Manufacturing (blades), Grex (pneumatic tools), Jorgensen® Clamp, Tru-Grip® Clamp, and Sommerfeld Tools For Wood.

I also want to thank the many persons whose support set this project into motion and provided resources to bring it to a successful completion: Helen Albert, Martin Miller, Wendi Mijal, Niki Palmer, Joseph and Anna Settich, Frank Siudowski, John F. Settich, Laura Greene, Cameron Robert Greene, Diane Beers, Otto and Audrey Beers, Louis and Mary Arth, Francis Siudowski, Mara Martinelli, and Barbara Settich.

CONTENTS

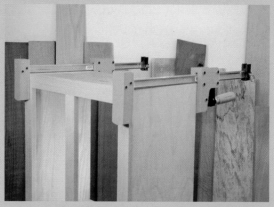

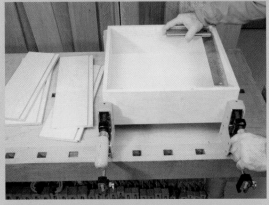

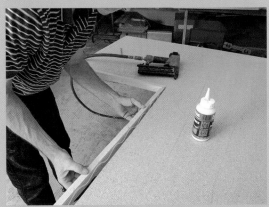

INTRODUCTION

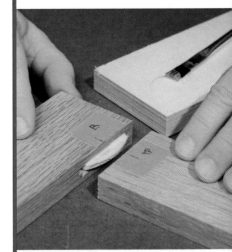

This book is your passport to the world of built-ins. It's a journey that can significantly add to your home's function, appeal, and value.

You'll enjoy "sightseeing tours" of completed projects, discovering concepts and details that will get your creative juices flowing. You'll also explore proven planning standards that will help you transform your ideas into a workable design. Then you'll discover advice on choosing materials as well as step-by-step photo sequences on building, fastening, and finishing every component in your built-in. Even the margins of this book work hard, delivering Pro Tips, Trade Secrets, and warnings about What Can Go Wrong.

But if you're short on tools or time, you'll see how you can benefit from the wide range of ready-made cabinets and other "off the shelf" components to give you professional-looking built-ins throughout your home. Even with a very humble tool kit and modest skills, you can confidently take on large projects.

And if the design process mystifies you, take advantage of the low cost service offered by several manufacturers. You can get a closet design, for example, at a surprisingly small fee.

And many home centers offer no-cost design consultation in the cabinetry department. Although kitchen and bath cabinets dominate the displays at these stores, many of the manufacturers featured there have broadened their output to include components for home offices and entertainment centers.

You'll also find that built-ins are often far easier and less expensive to make than a piece of furniture with a similar function. That's because a built-in usually doesn't have its sides, back, and top visible. So you can employ a utilitarian joinery and secondary woods instead of fussy joints and high-dollar lumber. In addition, a built-in can deliver plenty of cubic feet of storage, often without sacrificing square feet of living area. That's because you can make use of space that's currently wasted in areas with low vertical clearance, behind knee walls, and even in stud bays. As a result, you can minimize clutter and make your home live bigger than it is.

Whether your destination is a large or small built-in, this book will show you how to get there, making your project look right at home.

... when you can build permanent value into your home .
... other rooms in your home with functional, beautiful
... ions and accessories create comfortable and impressive
..., laundry areas, and more.

DESIGNING YOUR BUILT-IN

The design process for your built-in will simultaneously flow in two directions: from the outside inward, and from the inside outward. For example, suppose you want to flank a fireplace with bookcases extending to the adjacent walls. Because both the distance between the walls and the ceiling height define its maximum size, they affect its design from the outside inward.

At the same time, the items you'll store or display will help design the piece from the inside outward: setting the depth of the cabinets, determining the vertical spacing between shelves, guiding you in sizing drawers, and influencing the decision about whether the doors will have solid panels or glass.

In this chapter, you'll not only discover a practical approach to the planning process, you'll also learn about standard cabinet dimensions and how you can use ready-made cabinets to skip a lot of work. In addition, you'll find guidelines that will help you design cabinets, build shelves, maximize accessibility, create eating areas, and customize your closet. ▶ ▶ ▶

Understanding the Purpose of Your Built-in

To get the most satisfaction and usefulness from your built-in, you need to spend some time carefully considering its purpose. In fact, it's no exaggeration to say that the more time you invest in the design, the happier you'll be with the finished project.

The main function of most built-ins is storage, although the form it takes may be as simple as a wall niche holding a vase of flowers or as complex as an entertainment center brimming with the latest electronic technology.

Here are some of the storage options you can create with your built-in:

• **Display only.** This option can take several forms—the wall niche already mentioned, or a set of shelves for photographs, glassware, pottery, family memorabilia, or collectibles.

• **Display with open storage.** Using this option, you might combine shelving with storage behind glass, such as glass-front doors—in short, in a form that leaves the stored objects visible.

Closed storage, in drawers and behind opaque doors, conceals clutter while efficiently stowing your belongings.

• **Display with closed storage.** Closed storage means concealment in drawers or behind opaque doors. A built-in china cabinet would fall into this category if it has glass doors that show off glassware as well as paneled doors that hide serving pieces.

• **Closed storage only.** With everything hidden, you can maximize storage capacity because there's little need to artfully arrange the contents. This option would include a built-in dresser in a bedroom, a built-in linen closet with doors and drawers, or a built-in pantry in a kitchen.

Launching the plan

As a first step in the design process, make a list of all of the various items you want to store in your built-in, then separate them into categories depending on whether you want to display them in some form of open storage, hide them in closed storage, or house them in some combination of the two. Estimating the volume of space each group will occupy will help guide the scale, design, and appearance of your built-in.

Open storage, including shelving and glass-front doors, creates opportunities for displaying decorative items and keeping useful things close at hand.

Next, let's review some typical dimensions applied to cabinetry so you don't need to invent design standards from scratch. At this point, don't worry if your project needs to accommodate specialized items. We'll get into that topic right after we establish the general guidelines.

Cabinet standards

The drawing at right shows dimensions used widely throughout the cabinet industry, especially in kitchen and bath cabinets. Not surprisingly, these measurements tend to maximize the yield from standard sheets of plywood.

These sizes can serve as a starting point if you're designing your own built-ins, but the wide range of commercially available sizes and styles makes it easy to skip the cabinetmaking phase and jump ahead to the installation of custom-look built-ins.

Most cabinet manufacturers' brochures and websites show the full range of both their build-to-order and stock cabinet sizes. For example, one company's catalog offers 12-in.-deep wall cabinets in heights of 18 in., 24 in., 30 in., 36 in., and 42 in., with some units available in 1-, 2-, and 3-door configurations. Overall cabinet widths advance in 3-in. increments, making it easy to fit a run of cabinets between two walls without the need for wide filler strips.

You'll also find numerous cabinets for specialized purposes, such as rectangular blind wall cabinets for corner locations, angled corner cabinets with revolving shelves, and peninsula cabinets accessible from both sides. In addition, you'll find plenty of accessories, such as roll-out trays that maximize the usefulness and convenience of your cabinets.

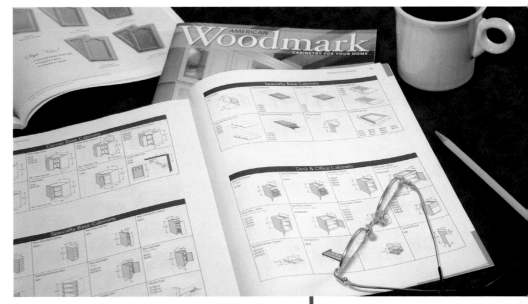

Cabinet manufacturers' catalogs display a wide inventory of sizes and configurations that may satisfy your needs for a built-in.

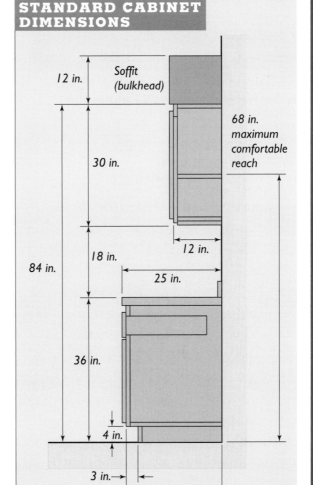

STANDARD CABINET DIMENSIONS

12 in. — Soffit (bulkhead)

68 in. maximum comfortable reach

30 in.

12 in.

84 in.

18 in.

25 in.

36 in.

4 in.

3 in.

24 in.

PRO**TIP**

Build a treasury
of design ideas by clipping pictures from magazines and catalogs. Stuff them into file folders along with your original sketches and notes.

A 36-in. countertop is usual for a standing kitchen work surface, but it would probably feel too high for a buffet, office credenza, or as part of an entertainment center. In those and other examples, a 30-in. height is more appropriate. You may be able to get the right height with a 24-in. wall cabinet set on a toekick and capped with your choice of countertop.

SAFETY FIRST

If shelves soar above the range of easy reach, provide a step stool or a library ladder. If a safe alternative isn't readily available, people will resort to antics such as stepping on shelves or standing on chairs.

Purchase prefinished cabinets, and you're on the fast track to completing a built-in project.

Making built-ins from standard cabinets

Some manufacturers have expanded beyond the kitchen and bath and are now building desk and office cabinets in the standard 24-in. depth but with a height of only 28½ in. Top a couple of such cabinets with a ready-made laminate countertop, and you have a nearly instant home office.

You can also create built-ins by adapting factory-made cabinets to new roles. For example, let's say you want a seating unit with storage for a mud room. Simply purchase a refrigerator-top wall cabinet that's 12 in. high, 24 in. deep, and in your choice of length: 30 in., 36 in., or 39 in. Set the cabinet on an easy-to-build toekick base, add a plywood top, and you're suddenly more organized.

Shelving heights

For both cabinets and open shelving, you'll maximize accessibility to contents when you consider the height of the person using them. The drawing "Maximum Reach Heights," below, illustrates the maximum comfortable reach heights for standing persons of average size. Easy browsing heights range from approximately eye level to the height of the waist. For shelves lower than that, a person will need to bend, crouch, or kneel.

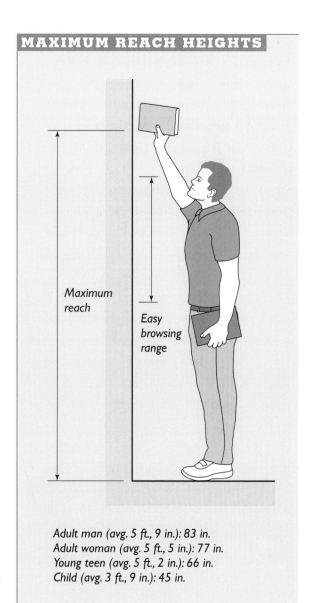

MAXIMUM REACH HEIGHTS

Maximum reach

Easy browsing range

Adult man (avg. 5 ft., 9 in.): 83 in.
Adult woman (avg. 5 ft., 5 in.): 77 in.
Young teen (avg. 5 ft., 2 in.): 66 in.
Child (avg. 3 ft., 9 in.): 45 in.

Dining and Table Standards

A built-in dining space can be reminiscent of a traditional hearthside inglenook or capture the styling of a '50s soda shop. But no matter what your décor goal, you'll want to make sure you're creating a comfortable space.

The drawing, "Dining and Table Standards," at right, gives you some starting guidelines for knee space, elbow room, and table height.

You'll note that 29 in. of side space per diner is considered standard. If you'll sometimes pull a chair to the free end of the table, add about 18 in. to its length, so a booth designed for two diners along the side and one at the end would be (2 x 29 in.) + 18 in. = 76 in.

When building a dining booth, avoid placing legs at the corners of the table: they can make it difficult to enter and exit. Instead, consider a wall-supported table, one or more pedestals, or a trestle design. To test the dimensions of your design, consider knocking together a quick mock-up from scrap or inexpensive materials

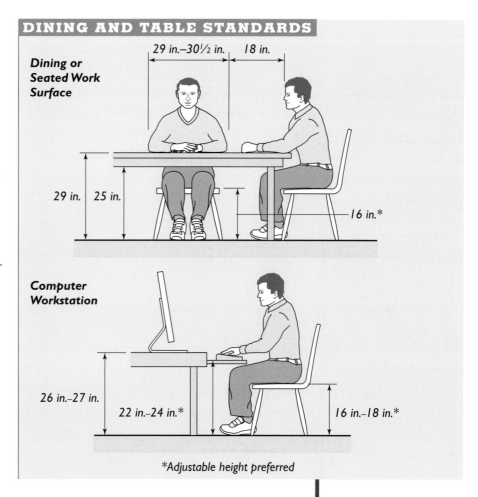

DINING AND TABLE STANDARDS

Dining or Seated Work Surface
29 in.–30½ in. 18 in.
29 in. 25 in. 16 in.*

Computer Workstation
26 in.–27 in.
22 in.–24 in.* 16 in.–18 in.*

*Adjustable height preferred

Designing for Accessibility

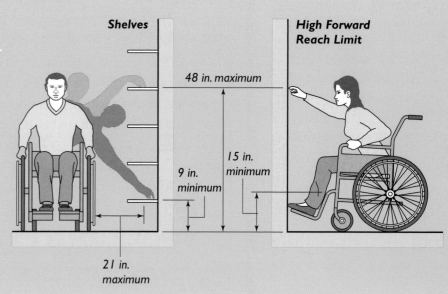

Shelves

High Forward Reach Limit

48 in. maximum

15 in. minimum

9 in. minimum

21 in. maximum

PRO TIP

As you refine the plans for your built-in dining booth, take a tape measure and notepad when you visit restaurants to record dimensions you find comfortable.

WHATCAN GOWRONG

Be cautious about making substantial deviations from standard dimensions to accommodate individuals. For example, tall homeowners may want built-ins tailored to their height. But prospective buyers may consider the built-ins out of scale and a serious drawback. It's more prudent to confine such customization to furniture—which is portable—instead of built-ins anchored to the house.

before committing to your good stock. Of course, another alternative is to order a custom-made booth. Most good-size cities have at least one fabricator that serves the restaurant trade.

Most desks and worktables share the same height as a dining surface, but computer stations tend to be shorter, and the keyboard tray is even lower. The combination of a keyboard shelf and chair that are both adjustable in height is a real plus, especially if several family members will share the computer station.

Buying bar stools

If your built-in includes a dining counter or bar, you'll need stools that elevate the seating above the 16-in. to 18-in. level considered standard for chairs. Although 30 in. is a common height for a bar stool, finding a comfortable perch involves a number of variables, including the elevation of the counter and the person's height.

The rule of thumb is that the top of the stool seat should be about 8 in. to 12 in. lower than the *bottom* surface of the counter. So if the top surface of the countertop is 36 in. high and is 1½ in. thick, the bar stool seat should be 22½ to 26½ in. high. For a 44-in.-high bar of identical

When you're choosing bar stools, one of the key dimensions is the height to the bottom of the counter.

thickness, the seating height should range from 30½ in. to 34½ in.

Most bar stools place the footrest about halfway between the seat and floor. For a person taller than 6 ft., 3 in., a rest at that position on a 30-in. stool becomes awkward. It pushes the knees too high for sustained comfort, yet the seat height prevents setting the feet on the floor. For that reason, tall individuals often find that a 36-in. stool is more comfortable when teamed with a counter height of 44 in. or more.

Short persons often face a similar dangling-leg dilemma on virtually every stool height. So choosing stools is definitely not a one-size-fits-all proposition.

Adjustable stools conquer many problems by allowing each person to select a comfortable height. For even further customization, some stools permit sliding the seating surface closer to the bar. Here's another tip: When you shop for bar stools with backs, look for those with a swivel that returns the seat to a preset position. This device provides a handy way to keep a room looking neat and organized without constantly fussing with the details.

Special-Item Storage

When you're entrusted with designing storage for valued collections, seek professional advice. Universities that teach library science, for example, can put you in touch with pros who know about optimal storage conditions for books and a wide range of recorded media. You can also talk to museum conservators who are responsible for items similar to the ones you'll be storing. Creating absolutely optimal archival conditions may be beyond your budget, but at the very least, you'll discover valuable advice about adverse conditions you can avoid.

Make sure you measure the size of the largest items when storing media. Many vary widely from "standard."

Locks are easy to install, and they help keep curious children (and nosy adults) from the contents of drawers and doors.

For example, light can fade many textiles, photos, and paper items. For these and similar pieces, the best preservation practice usually means dark and dry storage, which, of course, makes it hard to display and share a collection. As a compromise, consider locating the built-in completely out of direct sunlight, installing glass with ultraviolet protection, and rotating items from display to dark storage.

The design of built-ins whose function is to house a collection usually evolves from the inside out, with the size of the stored items driving the critical dimensions. Although the list at right provides some common dimensions of books and

recorded media, you should always double-check the size of the items you intend to store to be absolutely certain. For example, videotape cases vary in dimension, and large cases can add significantly to the space required.

Installing locks on some of the drawers and doors can discourage unauthorized access, but you don't want this to be your only line of security for a valuable collection. Depending on the value of your collection, you may want to consider deadbolt locks on entry doors, a whole-house security system, motion sensors, or other security devices.

Clothing: Storage Concepts

Clothing deserves special attention because apparel and accessories can represent a significant investment as well as a source of pride. For starters, pay attention to the temperature and quality of the air within your closet. If opening your closet door delivers a blast of heated or frigid air, consider increasing the closet's ventilation. Large walk-in closets need to be treated as living spaces with their own supply of conditioned air. If a walk-in closet is not as comfortable as the rest of your house, consult with your heating, ventilation, and air conditioning (HVAC) professional.

Closet basics

Most residential closets are about as basic as a builder could get away with: doors, a rod for clothes, and a shelf. That's probably just as well, because the best closets are personal spaces, customized to the clothes that reflect your lifestyle.

To start your closet organization, inventory the items you need to store. For example, some people are content with a few pairs of shoes, while others insist on having enough to keep a centipede well-shod. Count the number of

Standard Media Sizes

HERE ARE STANDARD DIMENSIONS FOR some common media items.

Small paperback book: 4¼ in. by 6⅞ in.

Standard hardcover book: 7 in. by 9½ in.

Large hardcover book: 9 in. by 14 in.

Atlas/large art book: 11 in. by 15 in.

DVD in case: 5⅜ in. by 7½ in.

VHS videotape (w/o case): 4⅛ in. by 7½ in.

Cassette tape: 2¾ in. by 4½ in.

PROTIP

Plan the closet layout so current clothing is in the most-accessible areas. Relegate out-of-season items to the less-handy corners and high shelves.

long hanging items such as overcoats and dresses, as well as short items, such as pants on a hanger, then design the space to accommodate everything.

The two basic styles of closets are the reach-in and the walk-in. While most of us generally consider walk-ins more luxurious, they can actually waste quite a bit of space because of the amount of floor area needed to navigate their interior. On the other hand, a properly designed reach-in closet can give you a highly efficient storage space with a place for everything you own.

Swapping out bypass doors for bifolds can make an immediate improvement in a reach-in closet because a reach-in closet allows you to see nearly all the contents at a glance. In addition, bypass doors increase the area available for drawers. Pocket doors are another option. On the plus side, they take up zero floor space. On the negative side, they can be balky performers.

Closet guidelines

• A walk-in closet should be at least 5 ft. deep to allow its door to swing inward and still allow sufficient hanging room on the back wall.

• Make your walk-in closet at least 11 ft. wide if you want to install a center island.

• In a walk-in closet, allow at least 2 ft. from the edges of the door to the side wall to permit hanging on these walls.

• For a reach-in closet, don't allow more than 18 in. from the door edges to the side wall of the closet. Otherwise, the corners become inaccessible.

• The optimum depth of a reach-in closet is 24 in. to 27 in. Additional depth doesn't yield usable space.

• Locate any light switches outside the closet. Choosing a switch with a pilot light makes it easy to confirm that you've switched off the bulb. Purchasing an inexpensive ceiling fixture looks better—and is safer—than a naked bulb.

• Use hooks—wall-mounted or on the back of a door—to store robes and "around the house" clothes.

• Label storage boxes or attach a photo of their contents.

DESIGNING AN EFFICIENT CLOSET

Double rods at 42 in. and 84 in.

Top shelf for off-season storage

Single rod 66 in. high

Space other shelves about 12 in. apart

Shoe shelves 7 in. apart

Shoe shelves 7 in. apart

Shoe shelves 7 in. apart

Bottom shelf 16 in. above floor

• Spacing shelves too far apart wastes space. Even for bulky items such as sweaters, about 12 in. is all you need. Keeping the bottom shelf about 16 in. above the floor allows room for boots and storage boxes under the shelf.

• For shoe storage, allow 7 vertical in. between shelves. To estimate storage capacity, allow about 9 in. of width per pair of men's shoes and 7 horizontal in. for a women's pair.

Hanging heights

• If your closet will feature a single shelf, set it about 66 in. above the floor and install the rod approximately 64 in. high. Before committing to this height—particularly if you're tall—make sure your long clothes won't drag on the floor. For double hanging, put the top bar 82 in. to 84 in. and the lower one 42 in. from the floor. This lower bar height also works well for a young child.

A well-organized closet rewards you with convenience every day. Make sure you give your shirts their typical 40 in. hanging length.

• Hang women's formal/full length gowns 78 in. or higher; bars for other long garments may be lowered to 68 in.

• Open-end pants hangers conserve space and are easier to use than the traditional design. Skirt hangers with clips are another convenient space-saver. Allow about 54 vertical in. from the bar to the floor for men's or women's slacks hung by the waist or cuff. Long skirts share this requirement. Pants folded over a hanger need only about 34 in. of hanging length.

Take Careful Planning Steps

AS YOU CONTINUE THE PLANNING process, try to stay on a methodical path instead of rushing to produce a finished design. Carefully measure the space you've chosen for your built-in, and do some loose sketches to determine whether the site will actually accommodate the use you have in mind.

One good technique is to challenge yourself to develop at least three different concepts for your project. You'll often find that your first idea isn't the best.

At this early stage, concentrate on the overall design, and don't get bogged down in the details of how to build it. Falling into that trap will suck all the creativity out of the process. Keep your sketches loose until you really feel that you're on the right track.

Next, shift to a more detailed rendering to scale, and that usually starts with an elevation (front view) of the project. As you refine that drawing, you'll find yourself also developing other views: side, top, and maybe even section drawings so you can explore and fully understand the design.

Frequently step back from the drawing board or computer to get a new viewpoint—this can often lead to fresh ideas. As you work, you'll find that many of the construction decisions will resolve themselves. And, with the majority of the design choices settled, you can now afford to switch from a highly creative mode into practical problem solving.

After you're satisfied with the design, make your hardware decisions. Drawer-slide hardware, for example, dictates clearances required for the drawer box.

Make a cutting list of all the parts, then use that to estimate the materials you'll need. For plywood parts, do a cutting diagram to ensure maximum yield from every sheet.

Now all that's left is the actual construction and installation.

DESIGN
OPTIONS

▲ An eating nook fit for five rests on a platform that helps create its own space separate from the cooking and prep areas.

▶ Don't overlook kitchen space as the perfect spot for a home office. With careful planning, countertops can do desk duty, too.

▲ Old-growth
quartersawn white
oak and quarter-
sawn French oak
veneer help create
a place to relax in
style. Latticework
on all of the cabinet
doors feature brass
pins that add an
eye-catching detail.

◄ Turned pomegranate
finials, chip-carved
"almonds," and carved
sunbursts are added
details that integrate
this cabinet with the
kitchen's turn-of-the-
century style.

▲ Window seats
are an especially
useful—and easy—
project for adding
both comfort and
storage space
at the ends of
narrow rooms
and landings.

MATERIALS

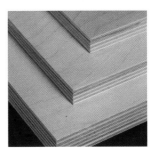

There are two kinds of people in this world: those who divide things into two categories and those who don't. In a similar way, you'll find two broad types of lumber for your built-in: solid wood and plywood. And you'll also find that each of these categories can also be neatly divided in two: softwoods and hardwoods.

But before you get the impression that lumber products exist in a strictly binary world, there's another large category of sheet goods you'll find at your lumber outlet. We'll review some of their strengths and weaknesses, both figuratively and literally. Some of these products have legitimate uses in your built-in projects, but I'll issue definite cautions about others.

In addition, you'll pick up some valuable tips that will help you get the most for your money when you buy materials. You'll also discover how to get smooth cuts in a wide range of materials and how to select glues that will keep your built-in solid for generations. ▶ ▶ ▶

Solid Wood

When you consider the enormous variety of trees covering the planet, it's amazing that the lumber they produce is classified into only two categories: hardwood and softwood. (To be technically correct, I should note that the ginkgo tree has its own classification, but you're not likely to make your built-in from this species.) Softwoods come from coniferous (evergreen) trees, most of which keep their foliage throughout the year, and hardwoods from deciduous trees, which usually shed their foliage each year.

The names soft- and hardwood are a bit unfortunate—lumber density doesn't really affect its classification. The densest softwood is more than four times harder than the softest hardwood.

Softwood lumber

Softwood lumber is marketed in a limited number of standard thicknesses, widths, and lengths. Its dimensions are often expressed as 1x or 2x, pronounced in conversation as "one-by" or "two-by," as with the familiar 2x4. These numbers represent the thickness and width of the lumber—its "nominal" or "real" dimensions at the rough-cut stage before shrinkage from drying and loss from final surfacing. The actual dimensions of softwood lumber are smaller than nominal. For example, a 1x4 actually measures about ¾ in. by 3½ in. Dimensional softwoods are sold in lengths of two-foot increments (6 ft., 8 ft., etc.), and here, their nominal and actual measurements closely agree.

The vast majority of softwood serves in a structural role, so its grading system reflects its strength, not appearance. However, your lumber dealer may have some "clear" softwoods, useful for making stain-grade trimwork and cabinet frames. In this context, "clear" means an absence of visually objectionable defects, such as knots.

Be aware that structural softwoods are usually air-dried instead of being kiln-dried. Kiln drying drives the moisture level down further and is generally reserved for furniture-grade hardwoods and expensive special-order softwoods. The high moisture content in air-dried softwood means it will shrink as it comes into equilibrium with the environment of your home. These dimensional changes usually don't present a practical problem unless you're building doors and other fit-critical components from air-dried softwoods. In these cases, minimize difficulties by consulting a book on properly conditioning the lumber.

Hardwood lumber

Like softwoods, most hardwoods are sold in standard thicknesses, though you'll find these thicknesses designated by a different nomenclature (see "Hardwood Lumber: The Quarter System" on p. 21).

Most hardwood is sold by the board foot in random widths and lengths. A board that is 1 in. thick, 12 in. wide, and 12 in. long contains a board foot, or 144 cubic in. So does a block measuring 2 in. by 4 in. by 18 in.

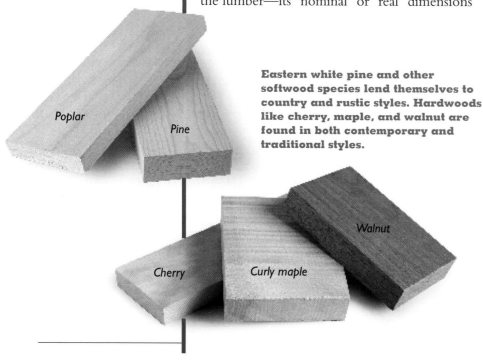

Eastern white pine and other softwood species lend themselves to country and rustic styles. Hardwoods like cherry, maple, and walnut are found in both contemporary and traditional styles.

Poplar

Pine

Walnut

Cherry

Curly maple

The board-foot system conserves a valuable commodity instead of creating waste in the name of uniformity. Most hardwood lumber is cut into custom sizes to get the largest possible number of usable pieces from each board. Structural softwoods are generally used in the widths as they come from the mill.

Here are the basic keys to buying hardwoods:

• Your species choice—white oak, walnut, or birch, for example—will largely be aesthetic. You'll want to match the look of the wood in your built-in to the style of its room. How the species accepts paint or varnish may also influence your choice (see "Finishing" on p. 132).

• Because hardwoods come in random lengths and widths, you'll need to develop a cutting list for the pieces in your project, visualizing how to cut them from the boards you select.

• Hardwood grades reflect its usable yield and the size of clear cuttings (cuttings without defects) you can obtain (see "Hardwood Lumber Grades" on p. 20).

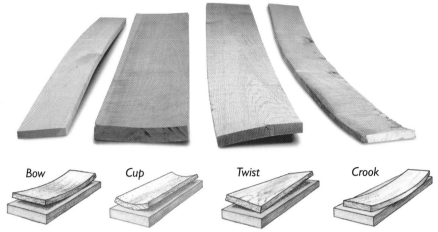

Bow   Cup   Twist   Crook

You may have trouble finding boards absolutely defect free. Workarounds exist for some defects, but in general, you want to purchase hardwoods as defect free as possible.

Hardwood lumber is sold in random lengths and widths. Avoid problems by cutting your largest components first.

What's a Board Foot?

A BOARD FOOT IS ANY COMBINATION of length, width, and thickness that when multiplied together results in a volume of 144 cubic inches. Formula for calculating board feet:
(l in. x w in. x h in. ÷ 144 = board feet)

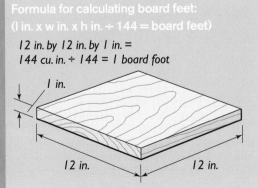

12 in. by 12 in. by 1 in. =
144 cu. in. ÷ 144 = 1 board foot

1 in.

12 in.   12 in.

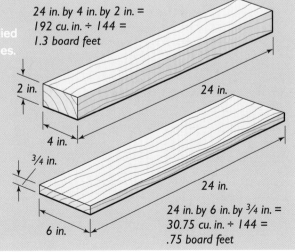

24 in. by 4 in. by 2 in. =
192 cu. in. ÷ 144 =
1.3 board feet

2 in.   24 in.

4 in.

3/4 in.

24 in.

24 in. by 6 in. by 3/4 in. =
30.75 cu. in. ÷ 144 =
.75 board feet

6 in.

• Certain species permit cosmetic shortcomings that don't affect the grade. For example, pitch pockets in cherry won't downgrade the lumber, even though you may want to eliminate them when cutting components for your project.

• Sapwood—the wood nearest the bark of the tree—may be lighter in color than the heartwood. But as long as it is sound, sapwood is usually not considered a defect. In some species, such as walnut, the contrast between sapwood and heartwood is dramatic. Trimming away all the sapwood could considerably increase your waste factor. If the change in tone doesn't fit the aesthetics of your project, limit your purchases to boards with consistent color tones.

• Dealers may charge a premium for scarce qualities, such as extra-wide boards or lumber with a fancy figure, such as bird's-eye maple.

Go figure

Many people confuse the terms "grain" and "figure" when referring to lumber. Grain refers to the direction of the wood fibers, and some of its related terms are "straight," "irregular," "wavy," "diagonal," "spiral," and "interlocked." In addition to its aesthetic qualities, grain direction is important when you're performing machining steps, such as routing, jointing, and thickness planing, because cutting in the wrong direction can lead to tearout.

Figure is the pattern produced by the grain, as well as other characteristics, like medullary rays, dormant buds, and stresses resulting from branches or external influences. Figure inspires a number of fanciful descriptive terms, such as "quilted," "fiddleback," "tiger," "bird's-eye," "flame," "feather," and many more.

Hardwood Lumber Grades

LUMBER IS A NATURAL MATERIAL and will contain defects that make certain parts of it unusable. Instead of looking for wood that's completely free of problems, visualize how many usable pieces a board will yield after you cut around the defects.

The higher the grade, the more expensive it is, but a higher grade will give you larger clear-cut pieces than a lesser grade. Insisting on the highest grade isn't always the most economical choice, however, because most built-ins require relatively small pieces. That can make it easy to work around the defects of a lower grade and save some money.

Here are the grades you'll find at your hardwood dealer:

Clear Face Cuttings: Free of defects, the highest grade of hardwood lumber, it can be somewhat difficult to find.

Firsts and Seconds (FAS): This grade yields 80 percent to 90 percent clear material and is the top one carried by most hardwood retailers.

First and Seconds one face (F1F): With about 83 percent of it's "good" side clear, this is a useful grade for cabinet components seen from only one side, such as face frames or false drawer fronts.

Selects: This is a category by itself, as well as the starting point for a classification some dealers called "Selects and Better."

Below this, you're getting into wood more suited to hidden applications. You can still get some clear cuttings from these lower grades, but they get smaller and the waste ratio becomes huge. The grades continue with No. 1 Common, No. 2A Common, No. 3A Common, Sound Cuttings, No. 2B Common, No. 3B Common, and Sound Wormy.

Sapwood (the lighter colored wood of this cherry board) can offer pleasant contrasts, but may require special finishing to blend it with the other wood tones.

This quartersawn white oak displays a handsome and desirable ray pattern.

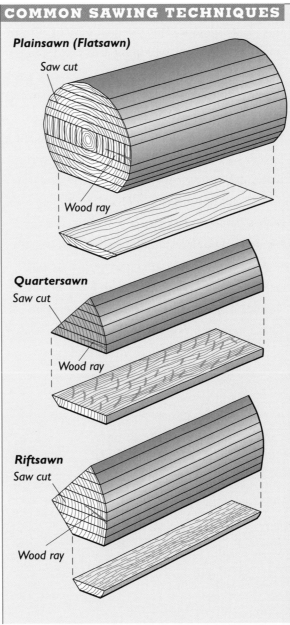

Plainsawn (Flatsawn)
Saw cut
Wood ray

Quartersawn
Saw cut
Wood ray

Riftsawn
Saw cut
Wood ray

WHAT CAN GO WRONG

Some mills surface 4/4 lumber to $^{13}/_{16}$ in., but others take it down to $^{25}/_{32}$ in. In addition, some mills surface rift- and quartersawn materials $^{1}/_{32}$ in. thinner than plainsawn. Be aware of these potential variations, especially if you incorporate material from several sources.

A sawmill operator can't change the wood grain, but decisions made at cutting time definitely influence the appearance of its figure. Here are three common sawing methods.

Plainsawn lumber, also known as flatsawn or through-and-through cutting maximizes the yield from the log, and many of the boards display the familiar cathedral figure, named for its similarity to the shape of a church roof. This cutting method will also produce a few boards that appear quartersawn or riftsawn.

Quartersawn lumber begins by slicing the log into four segments, then slicing the boards at right angles to the annual rings, as indicated in the drawing at right. Woods with a prominent structure of medullary rays will then reveal a striking figure called "flake" or "ray." Compared to plainsawing, quartersawing consumes more energy and also reduces yield. These factors, plus the desirability of the figure, make quartersawn lumber more expensive.

Hardwood Lumber: The Quarter System

Quarters	Rough Thickness (in.)	Hardwoods Planed S2S (in.)
3/4	$^{3}/_{4}$	$^{9}/_{16}$
4/4	1	$^{13}/_{16}$
5/4	$1^{1}/_{4}$	$1^{1}/_{16}$
6/4	$1^{1}/_{2}$	$1^{5}/_{16}$
8/4	2	$1^{3}/_{4}$

Lumber Lingo

EVERY TRADE HAS ITS OWN abbreviations, and if you know them you'll be OK, but if not, you're SOL.

AD = Air-dried lumber

BF = Board foot

KD = Kiln-dried lumber

LF = Lineal foot, sometimes also called running foot. Applies to products that are sold by length, particularly when they're produced in random lengths, such as hardwood moldings.

RL&W = Random lengths and widths, describing the common method of marketing hardwood lumber.

S2S = Surfaced two sides, meaning that the lumber has been jointed and thickness planed on two sides to a consistent dimension. Edges are generally rough-cut or have the natural edge of the tree.

S4S = Surfaced four sides, describing lumber whose parallel faces and edges are surfaced. Hardwood lumber that receives these extra machining steps sells at a premium compared to S2S.

SF = Square foot; usually applies more to sheet goods instead of lumber.

SLR = Straight-line ripped, meaning that one edge has been cut straight. However, you should freshly joint an SLR surface prior to edge-gluing.

SLR1E = Straight-line ripped one edge; means the same as SLR.

Riftsawn lumber also begins with a log cut into four segments. But several differences distinguish it from quartersawing. The sawmill operator places the log at an angle that reduces waste and produces wider stock with a characteristically regular and straight figure. Although you may consider this figure bland, the understated restraint of a riftsawn figure may keep attention focused on the overall architecture of the piece.

Hardwood lumber thickness

Hardwood lumber employs a system of quarter inches to express thickness of the roughsawn lumber. Once surfaced, the boards are, of course, thinner. The chart, "Hardwood Lumber: The Quarter System," on p. 21, lists typical thicknesses you'll encounter, although you'll find subtle variations from one dealer to another.

To use the language of this system, don't pronounce the measurements as fractions. Instead, you say, "six quarter," for example.

The quarter system usually doesn't apply to softwoods, though it's increasingly common to see softwood decking marketed as 5/4 stock, with a finished thickness of about 1 in.

Plywood

Plywood gets its name from the fact that it's made by gluing together a number of thin layers, or plies, of wood. The manufacturer lays the grain of the plies at right angles to each other, producing a sheet that's dimensionally stable. That means its size changes very little in response to fluctuations in atmospheric humidity, a valuable characteristic for built-in carcases. In addition, plywood sags less in spans than solid lumber, making it well suited for shelving (see "Shelves" on p. 54 for more information).

We'll take a look at two categories of plywood that you'll find useful in creating built-ins: hardwood ply and Baltic birch. We'll skip a discussion of softwood plywood because its construction is the same as hardwood ply, only with softwood faces, and with a few exceptions, it's generally not suited for visible components.

When you choose softwood plywood, you'll note the appearance of the veneers are graded on an alphabetical scale, with "A" having the best looks. Both sides are graded, and the double-letter grade is stamped on the rear face. You can choose panels laminated with either interior or exterior glues—the word "exterior" on the grade stamp indicates an exterior-rated adhesive.

Hardwood ply: Veneers

Some of the big-box home centers carry a limited selection of plywoods faced with hardwood veneers, and their quality can often be marginal. Because the big-box business model is generally based upon offering products with wide market

From left to right, curly maple, quilted maple, and ribbon-stripe mahogany are just a few of the dramatic figures veneered products offer for your built-ins.

appeal at a low price, you'll find that quality improves and selection broadens when you visit a hardwood lumber dealer.

In addition to choosing species and finishes, when you buy hardwood ply you should consider the arrangement of the face veneers and the construction of the core. (If your project calls for paint, by the way, consider birch plywood. It accepts paint very nicely.) Be cautious when buying oak, so you (or the dealer) don't accidentally mix white and red oak together.

The arrangement of the veneer on the sheet has a huge influence on its appearance, as you can see in the drawings at right.

Rotary-cutting is the least expensive manufacturing method. Mounting a log on a giant lathe and spinning it against a knife produces a continuous peeling, somewhat like the continuous sheet you'd pull from a roll of wrapping paper. On the negative side, the resulting figure (grain pattern) usually doesn't resemble anything you'd see on a piece of solid lumber. Some woodworkers find the effect so distracting they absolutely refuse to buy plywood with rotary-cut veneers for any visible parts of a project.

PLYWOOD VENEER PATTERNS

Rotary

Book-Matched
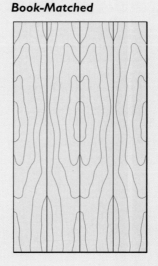

Slip-Matched
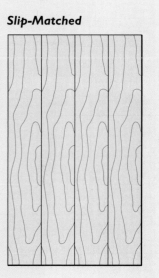

Slicing produces extremely thin sheets of wood. Depending on how the log is mounted, the resulting veneer can resemble the appearance of plainsawn, riftsawn, or quartersawn lumber. As they're cut, the millworker stacks the sheets in the order they came from the log. If the mill worker flips every other sheet when laying the face veneer, the result is a pair whose pattern appears as nearly a mirror image. Because the laying motion is like opening pages of a book, such a pattern is called "bookmatched." Each

Hardwood Plywood Grades

Face	Veneer Quality	Defects Permitted
A	Sliced veneer may be either bookmatched or slipmatched. Rotary-cut veneer in a single piece is permissible.	Small pin knots and burls are allowed, but not in excessive amounts. Tiny patches allowed.
B	Sliced veneer need not be matched, but there cannot be great contrasts in color or figure.	In addition to defects above, burls and slight color streaks are allowed.
C	Face must be sound, with no unpatched defects. Small areas of rough grain are permitted.	In addition to defects above, there may be unlimited color variations and streaks.
D	Face must be sound, with no open defects. The percentage of permissible rough grain area varies among species.	(Same as for grade C.)

Back	Veneer Quality	Defects Permitted
1	Open defects not permitted. Grain match and color consistency are not required.	Smooth patches, small sound and tight knots, and discoloration allowed.
2	Every defect must be repaired	Knots permitted but must be sound and tight.
3	Face must be generally sound, with some open defects allowed.	In addition to defects above, knotholes and repaired splits are permitted.
4	Low-grade veneer, sometimes called reject material.	In addition to defects above, major discoloration and knotholes up to 4-in. diameter permitted.

sheet looks natural, and their symmetry increases their attractiveness. Bookmatching is the most popular veneer pattern on quality hardwood lumber.

If the mill worker applies each veneer face without flipping it, the result is called slip-matched. Slipmatched plywood is quite scarce, and that's a good thing as far as many people are concerned: they feel this method produces a monotonous or striped effect.

Hardwood ply: Grades

Each side of a plywood panel carries its own appearance grade, and the requirements of your project will guide your selection. For example, if you're buying material for drawer bottoms or the back of a carcase, only one side needs to be attractive. In that case, you can economize by buying plywood with a low-quality back. But if you're purchasing material for door panels, which will be seen from both sides, you'll want no objectionable defects on the back. As you can see from the chart at left, the face grades are lettered and the back grades are numbered.

Hardwood ply: Cores

Hardwood plywoods come with many different kinds of cores, but that doesn't mean you'll find all of them at every dealer. Instead, you'll be limited pretty much by the kind of core each dealer offers, so if you prefer a different core, you'll probably need to find a different retailer.

Veneer core, built with sheets of thick veneers that alternate grain directions, is the most widespread type of plywood core. To get an idea of its quality, check the edges of the panel for voids in the core. Ideally, there should be no voids because the face veneer could sag into a hidden hole, creating a dish-shaped depression.

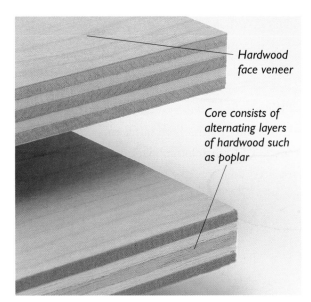

Veneer-core construction is a typical assembly method for both soft- and hardwood plywoods.

The edges and ends of veneer-core plywood make good gluing surfaces, and the panel provides a good target for mechanical fasteners.

Lumber core has a heart of edge-glued wood strips with crossbanded veneer layers above and below it. The long grain edges make a good gluing surface, but end-grain surfaces are considerably weaker. Screws and nails hold well.

Composite core uses a veneer center sandwiched between layers of high-density particleboard. The particleboard produces a smooth surface for the face veneers, and the edges and ends usually offer decent gluing strength. Fasteners in the central veneer core hold well, but you'll probably get better strength by selecting screws suitable for particleboard.

Particleboard or flakeboard cores offer economy and a smooth substrate for face veneers. On the downside, they offer little strength in spans, so you'll need to engineer any shelves with aprons to gain decent load-carrying ability. In addition, you'll find that it's difficult to get chip-free cuts with these materials. Gluing can also be a challenge because the edges and ends don't make high-quality gluing surfaces. Choose screws carefully to achieve strength without splitting.

Fiberboard or MDF cores also offer economy and a smooth substrate for face veneers, but they exhibit low span strength and make gluing and the use of mechanical fasteners challenging. However, you'll find that these cores cut more cleanly than particleboard or flakeboard.

Baltic birch plywood

Baltic birch, which sometimes goes by the alias of "Russian birch," is an attractive light-colored plywood that's widely used for drawer sides and bottoms. The thin plies employed in its construction and the lack of voids give the edges and ends a more tailored look than domestic panels. The usual sheet size is approximately 60 in. by 60 in.

Because Baltic birch is a European product, it follows European, not American, standards, so ask your dealer the specific grade(s) he or she carries. Here's a brief summary of those grades.

Baltic birch ply, available in a number of thicknesses, has a better-looking edge appearance than most veneer-core plywoods.

WHAT CAN GO WRONG

Sometimes you absolutely need top-quality veneers on both sides of a plywood sheet, but your dealer may not stock suitable material. Even if your dealer will special-order for you, you may be subject to a minimum quantity that is far more than you need, and you may also be hit with hefty handling fees.

Skip the hassle by making your own premium panels. For example, face-gluing the "imperfect" veneers of two ¼-in. sheets will give you a ½-in. panel whose 'A' veneers look great from both sides.

A glue bond can last as long as the wood itself, but glue has a limited lifespan in its container: usually about two years from the date of manufacture. In addition, glue exposed to temperature extremes produces weak joints. Some glues clearly note their expiration date, but others print an encoded batch number on the bottle. Visit the manufacturer's website or call the customer service number for information to crack the code. Never use glue that that's turned thick or stringy because you'll get weak joints.

The **"B" face grade** is the highest, and features a one-piece rotary-cut veneer face that's usually light and even in color. Small brown streaks and pin knots may be present, but there are no patches or mineral streaks.

The **"BB" face** is the next-highest grade, and it permits sound tight knots and mineral streaking. Color-matched football-shaped patches replace open knots.

The **"C" grade** permits veneer splits, open knots, and patches. The surface is not sanded.

Other sheet goods

A few more panel materials merit mention. Some you'll find useful, but others deserve strong cautions. The typical sheet size for most of these materials is 48 in. by 96 in. However, you find a few panels now come a full inch wider and longer, and this additional size simplifies calculations. For example, a wider sheet enables you to slice it into four 12-in. pieces. This feat is impossible with a 48-in. panel because of waste created by the width of the sawblade.

Hardboard (Masonite® is one common brand), made from wood fiber, wax, and resins, is a grainless panel that's an economical choice for painted or hidden carcase backs, drawer bottoms, and a few other parts of a built-in project. Two common thicknesses are ⅛ in. and ¼ in. The standard panel is usually a light tan color, with one smooth and one textured surface. It cuts relatively cleanly, though the back side of the cut usually exhibits some fuzziness along the edges. Tempered hardboard has a darker color and is stronger, slightly more expensive, and cuts more cleanly. Some manufacturers produce panels with a factory-applied finish in a range of colors.

Melamine-covered panels are a real time saver because they eliminate finishing chores.

Baltic birch panels

Thickness (mm)	Thickness (in.)*	Number of plies
3	⅛	3
6	¼	5
9	⅜	7
12	½	9
15	⅝	11
18	¾	13

* Inch equivalency nominal and approximate.

Here's a selection of inexpensive sheet goods that you may choose as part of your built-in project: melamine panel, hardboard, and MDF.

You'll find these panels with the shelf-pin holes already bored, saving even more time and effort.

Particleboard and oriented strand board (OSB) are inexpensive panels that have many uses in the construction industry, but they're not well suited to built-in projects, even as hidden components. Particleboard is nearly as vulnerable to water as the Wicked Witch of the West. Although it doesn't immediately dissolve like the Witch, this material swells, then disintegrates.

Medium density fiberboard (MDF) is a dimensionally stable material that machines cleanly, making it valuable for painted components such as raised panels and moldings.

You can also use it for carcases and other components that you'll cover with laminate. MDF has little span strength, so you'll need to beef up shelves with aprons or another engineering solution. Common thicknesses are ¼ in., ½ in., and ¾ in. The latter makes a great substrate for laminate countertops (see "Countertops" on p. 108). Oversized sheets, 49 in. by 97 in., are relatively common. And you may want an exterior grade (Medex® is one brand name) for a substrate when you're installing a sink.

Medium density overlay (MDO) is an exterior plywood panel clad with a weather-resistant resin overlay. You probably won't employ MDO in a built-in project, but it makes an excellent material for forming a concrete countertop. Unlike plywood, MDO won't transfer grain and patches to the concrete. Instead, it leaves a smooth matte surface.

Wood Glue

There are truly an astonishing number of woodworking glues on the market, and so it's easy for the beginner to become confused. I've tried quite a number of different glues, but I stick with those that have given me excellent results:

Titebond® III is an excellent general-purpose adhesive that will produce water-resistant bonds stronger than the wood itself. You can purchase yellow glue that's not water-resistant, but it's only slightly less expensive.

White glue offers a longer open time than yellow woodworkers' glue, stretching the opportunity to position parts before the adhesive grabs. This is a great glue to utilize for complex assemblies. Even after it's cured, water or excessive humidity can dissolve white glue, so keep it away from potentially damp locations.

Liquid hide glue also offers a long open time. One of its other great virtues is that it will not block absorption of stain or clear finish, so you eliminate the problem of light blotches that can result from incomplete cleanup of other glue types. This glue has a distinctive aroma that some people may find objectionable, and it's also subject to the effects of moisture in humid rooms.

Molding and trim glue is a thick-body formula that reduces dripping. It provides high initial tack without grabbing too aggressively so you can reposition parts if necessary. The fact that it dries clear is another plus.

Melamine glue is specially formulated to bond melamine to wood, MDF, particleboard, and other porous substrates, high-pressure laminate, and even metal. This glue produces a strong initial tack, but still gives you enough working time for accurate alignment. One tip: Before using it, be sure to shake or stir the glue to ensure a uniform consistency.

These five glues, Titebond III, liquid hide glue, melamine glue, white glue, and molding and trim glue, will handle almost any challenge in assembling and installing built-ins.

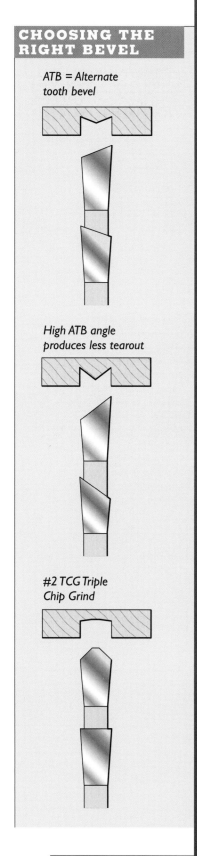

*ATB = Alternate
tooth bevel*

*High ATB angle
produces less tearout*

*#2 TCG Triple
Chip Grind*

Making Clean Cuts

Even the best plans and finest materials for your built-in won't mean much if your sawblade scorches solid lumber and splinters veneers. A well-tuned saw and blades that are both clean and sharp will minimize these problems. A zero-clearance tablesaw insert (see p. 77) is another effective strategy for minimizing tearout.

But it's also important to choose blades specifically engineered for the material and cutting chore. And consider your tablesaw's power when choosing blades. Thin-rim blades make a narrower cut and can maximize the limited horsepower of contractor-style saws, but the thicker body of a standard-kerf blade improves running stability. The recommended blades listed here are all carbide-tipped:

• 40-tooth ATB 10-in. combination rip and crosscut tablesaw blade. ATB means "alternate tooth bevel," which slopes successive teeth in opposite directions in a clean, shearing action. This workhorse blade will handle virtually all of your solid-lumber cutting chores and also produce clean rip cuts in veneered plywood.

• 80-tooth high-AT 10-in. tablesaw blade. High-AT (also called high-ATB) means the alternate tooth bevel is ground at a more pronounced angle: 40 degrees is typical. This steeper slope produces a shearing action that minimizes tearout, even on the back side of demanding materials such as melamine panels and oak plywood.

• 80-tooth ATBR 10-in. mitersaw blade. If your saw takes 12-in. blades, choose a 100-tooth pattern. The ATBR pattern has four teeth in the ATB grind followed by a flat-top raker tooth that pulls waste from the kerf to prevent burn-

Purchase high-quality blades, and keep them clean and sharp to achieve smooth results.

ing. If you work with polystyrene moldings, this blade may melt the material. If that happens, get a blade specifically engineered for this material.

• 80-tooth #2 TCG 10-in. blade for your tablesaw. The #2 TCG is a variety of the triple chip grinding pattern. This is a specialized blade that will minimize splintering when you're slicing sheets of high-pressure laminate to rough dimensions. This blade also gives you smooth cuts in cast acrylic sheets that you may want to utilize in doors instead of glass. If you don't want to invest in this blade, put your 80-tooth mitersaw blade into your tablesaw when slicing laminate sheets.

• An 8-in. stack-dado set for your tablesaw equips it to cut dadoes, grooves, rabbets, and other joints. Purchase plastic or metal shims, placing them between the cutters when you need to fine-tune the width. Years ago, I used a "wobble" style of dado head, but at some widths the bottom of the groove curved noticeably. In addition, the stack set produces cleaner edge cuts.

Hardwoods and softwoods are merely a starting point in molding choices. You'll also find plastics and wood composites

Molding

Sometimes moldings are primarily practical, hiding the raw edge of plywood, for example, or covering a gap between the side of your built-in and the wall. Other times, their principal purpose is decorative, their curves or angles speaking an element of the stylistic vocabulary. At their best, moldings are profiles with a purpose—they perform a function, but do it with flair.

Molding Choices

When you shop for moldings at a "big box" retailer, you'll find a wide range of profiles and materials. Softwood moldings classified as "stain grade" should come free of knots and other defects that would show under a clear finish. "Paint grade" moldings are considerably less expensive, and are often made of short pieces of finger-jointed lumber. The joints are invisible under paint, and some sport a factory-applied primer, saving you time and materials.

Then there are prefinished moldings made with a decorative skin applied to a plastic or wood-composite substrate. White plastic moldings used in a "white" design environment can eliminate a painted topcoat, but they accept a finish well if you want to match their color to decorative elements. In addition, plastic can mimic elaborate decorative moldings at a fraction of the cost of a hand-carved original.

Home centers usually have a limited selection of hardwood moldings. For a special profile or species a specialty lumber yard or local custom cabinet shop are better sources.

Then too, consider decorative corbels and wood appliqués. Corbels can play a structural as well as a decorative role, supporting a shelf or countertop. Staining an appliqué of one species to match the wood of your built-in can be a difficult challenge, but using them on a painted piece is an easy task.

Making your own moldings

Purchasing hardwood moldings can get expensive quickly, and locating species other than red oak can be a real challenge. Fortunately, it's fairly easy to rout moldings in your own shop. You can also make more complex shapes by combining several different cuts on a single molding. Other tools useful for this task are a shaper and a table-saw molding head with interchangeable cutters.

1. Joint the edge of a board at least 2 in. wide square and straight, and chuck the bit into your table-mounted router. Set up a fence flush with the bearing on the bit (if it has one), and cut the profile into the edge of the board, as shown in Photo **A**. When removing a lot of wood, make a series of progressively deeper cuts by either elevating the bit or adjusting the fence till the bearing is flush with it.

SAFETY FIRST

If your home was built before 1978, its paint may contain lead. To find out for certain, you can purchase an inexpensive test kit at paint stores and home centers.

Lead paint may not be a problem unless the paint chalks or flakes off, or if you disturb the finish by sanding or scraping. If you're removing lead-painted molding for reuse, sending it a professional stripper may be the safest strategy. To discover more about lead paint safety, visit the website of the United States Environmental Protection Agency: www.epa.gov/lead/.

Standardized Moldings

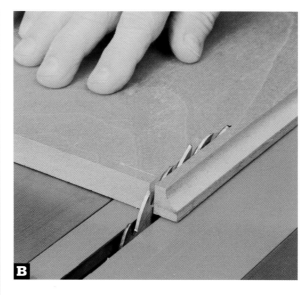

2. Cut the profile strip free from the board on your tablesaw. If possible, position the profile outside of the blade so it falls away from the blade as shown in Photo **B**. A strip caught between the blade and fence represents a kickback hazard.

Removing and reusing moldings

The demolition phase of a project isn't simply about applying brute force. Finesse has its place, too. With a little bit of care, you can remove moldings intact and reuse them.

SAFETY FIRST

Never try to shape a profile on a narrow strip of wood. Narrow stock is too difficult to control, and even a momentary snag on the cutter could shatter the workpiece. Instead, mold the profile into the edge of a wider board and then cut the profile free.

1. If there's paint or caulk between the molding and the wall, slice through it with a utility knife. Go slowly; don't nick the molding. Next, work a slim-bladed 4-in. putty knife between the molding and wall. Gently pull forward on the handle to increase the gap between the molding and wall, as shown in Photo **C**. One key throughout this process is to spread pressure over a wide area, minimizing potential damage.

2. In stubborn situations, you can tap softwood shims behind the blade, as shown in Photo **D**. When your putty knife reaches a nail, setting shims on either side of the fastener will give you a definite advantage.

3. When you've developed a wide enough gap at a nail location, slip in a thin prybar or molding removal tool between the back of the molding and the putty knife and lever against the back of the molding instead of along a visible edge, as shown in Photo **E**. The putty knife spreads the pressure on the wall, but continue to work gently to avoid damage. Continue to work along the wall, prying at the nail locations. Don't pry between the nails—you'll bend the molding and risk breaking it. Don't pry the molding completely loose at one nail. Work back and forth to avoid splitting the wood.

Making Molding Joints

Three basic cuts will handle virtually all of your molding needs.

You'll use a **square cut** for butting against a wall or where one type of molding meets another—at the junction of a baseboard and the edge of a door jamb, for example.

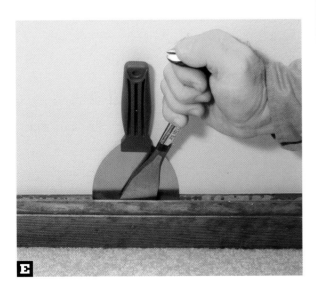

Miters are for outside corners, and this joint usually requires mirror-image angles cut in both pieces.

A **cope cut** handles inside corners.

Marking square cuts

A square cut is absolutely uncomplicated when you've tuned up your mitersaw so the blade is square to both the fence and the table (see p. 73 for the squaring procedure). At casing junctures, I like to mark crosscuts by overlapping the molding, holding a sharp utility knife square to the casing, and pressing down, as shown in the photo below. This method is especially handy for molding you intend to finish before installing it, when a pencil line could be difficult to see.

Learning to miter

1. To miter a joint, begin by measuring the angle of the outside corner, using a protractor at least 12 in. long to get past any drywall compound humped at the corner. Photo **A** on p. 32 shows two measuring tools: the plastic True Angle® from Quint is reasonably priced

Forget the tape measure when you can scribe the cutline directly on the molding. Press straight down on your utility knife.

A

When you're removing window or door casings, look for fasteners that cross the mitered corners. Prying at right angles to them could split the molding.

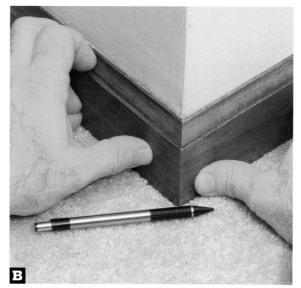
B

C

and very easy to use. The electronic Miterfinder from Bosch® is a bit pricey but its big digital readout automatically calculates miter and bevel settings for crown molding. It's well worth considering if you'll do any volume of crown installation.

2. After you've measured the angle, divide it in half to determine each miter angle. Cut both the right and left halves of the joint, and then test-fit the pair, as shown in Photo **B**. If you're painting the molding, you can hide an imperfect joint with putty, but clear finishes require more care and finesse.

3. Apply a thick-bodied molding glue to the miter joint and nail the pieces in place, as shown in Photo **C**. For more information on fastening tools and techniques, see p. 124 and the sidebar "Tougher Than (Ordinary) Nails" on p. 35.

Learning to cope

1. One half of a cope cut is very easy—simply butt one length of molding into a corner. Coping the other half removes the shape of the molding profile from the end of the other piece, which allows that end to fit snugly over the first piece, even in out-of-square situa-

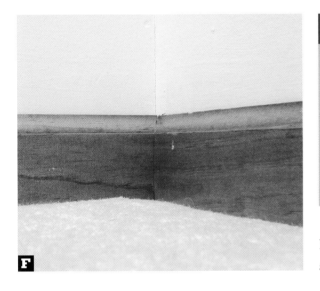

tions. Begin the cope cut by slicing a 45-degree miter, then clamp the piece securely to your workbench. As shown in Photo **D**, tilt the coping saw to produce a slight undercut, and saw along the profile of the miter cut.

2. Until you gain confidence in your coping saw skills, it's prudent to stay just shy of the waste side of the line, and then clean up the edge with a sharp utility knife, as shown in Photo **E**.

3. Sliding the coped cut against the installed molding should produce a snug fit, as shown in

Photo **F**. If necessary, use your utility knife or a rasp to fine-tune the cope.

Crown molding: A special case

Installing crown follows the same general principles as other moldings, but the fact that it's installed at an angle calls for a compound miter, which somewhat complicates the procedure.

1. With a compound mitersaw you can cut the molding flat, but remembering which way to angle and tilt the blade for each cut can pose a challenge. Avoid the confusion by making yourself a set of templates similar to those shown in Photo **A** on p. 34.

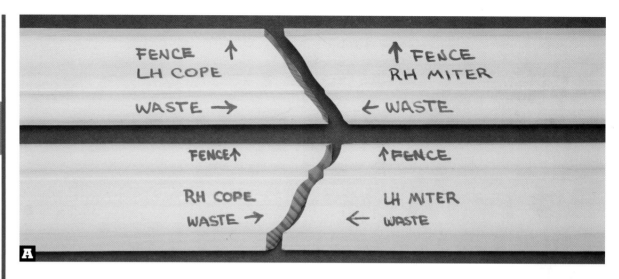

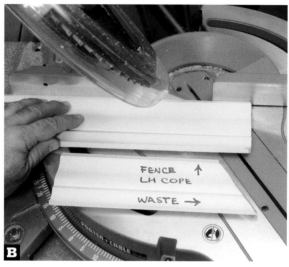

2. Measure the angle of the outside corner and then consult a miter-and-bevel chart—your mitersaw almost certainly came packed with one. Make sure the chart matches the spring angle of the molding you're installing (see "Know the Spring Angle" on the facing page), and lock the saw settings. (The Bosch Miterfinder calculates the miter and bevel settings and displays them.) To verify the setup, place the correct template on the saw table, as shown in Photo **B**, then make the cut. Installation is similar to flat miters: Apply glue to the cut edges and nail in place.

3. Another approach relies on the Cut-N-Crown jig shown in Photo **C**. You simply refer to the pictorial directions to orient the stock on the jig: for example, face down and bottom downward for a right miter. The saw's angle setting is one-half of the corner angle, but you never bevel the blade. In addition, you make all of the cuts with the jig on the left side of the blade. It's a clever tool that dramatically reduces saw setup time between cuts. There are three jigs, manufactured to match the common spring angles of crown molding: 38 degrees, 45 degrees, and 52 degrees. The spring angle of the molding you're installing, of course, dictates the jig you'll use.

Matching Vintage Moldings

IN SOME OLDER HOMES, THE ANTIQUE millwork can act as a distinctive design element that unites your new built-in with the rest of the home. But you may run into a serious problem when you take a sample of the old profile to a modern lumberyard. If it was a production molding, it may have been discontinued long ago. Or it may have been custom-made by the finish carpenter using a molding plane with a single blade or by slicing a succession of profiles with several different blades.

There are alternate strategies that may solve this problem. Check with your neighbors, and you may find yourself pleasantly surprised to discover someone with several pieces of matching molding cluttering the attic. Architectural salvage yards are another potential source. Next, check with local millwork shops—they may already keep cutters on hand that could duplicate your molding. As a last resort, you could order a set of custom shaper cutters, then engage a shop to mill the molding for you. If you make the investment in the cutters, take them with you when the job is completed in case you ever need the profile again.

Tougher Than (Ordinary) Nails

WHEN YOU'RE WORKING WITH DENSE materials, such as trim or hardwood, you may want to try hard trim nails (sometimes also called hard finish nails). They get a special heat treatment at the mill to make them more bend resistant, and they can save you a lot of frustration. You may even be able to skip the tedious step of drilling pilot holes in the trim.

Beware of "bargain" hard trim nails, because those fasteners can retain an oily residue your hands will quickly transfer to the molding. The oil causes finishing problems on bare wood and spoils the appearance of trimwork you've already finished.

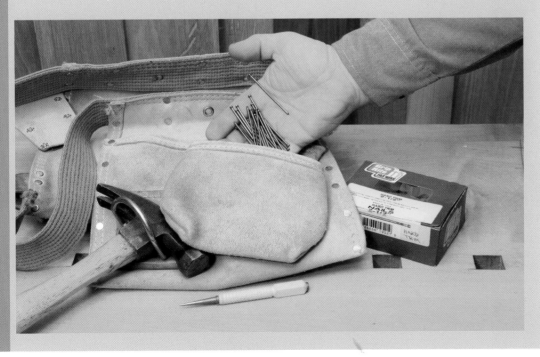

Know the Spring Angle

THE SPRING ANGLE IS THE angle measured between the back of the molding and the wall. In the illustration below it's 38 degrees. The complementary angle of 52 degrees describes the slope of the molding to the floor. This molding is often referred to as 52/38 crown, and is probably the most common type. However, you may encounter 45-degree crown as well, and a spring angle of 52 degrees.

52/38 Crown

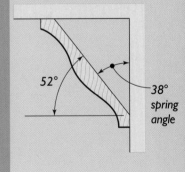

52°

38°
spring
angle

CARCASE ASSEMBLY STRATEGIES

As its name implies, a cabinet's carcase is its body, serving as the basic structure to which you add the other components, such as doors, drawers, and perhaps a countertop. Except for an occasional visible end panel, most of the carcase is usually concealed, especially in built-in projects. As a result, the doors and drawers assert the style of the cabinetry.

But even though the carcase doesn't have the outgoing personality of a drawer or door doesn't mean it's unimportant. Compare a carcase to the foundation of a house, and you'll understand its importance. A carcase must be square and sturdy so doors fit properly and drawers slide sweetly.

In this chapter, we'll explore methods of building both face-frame and frameless styles of carcases, and we'll also discuss how the construction strategy interrelates with the installation process. Along the way, we'll touch on two other time-and labor-saving options: purchasing finished cabinets and modifying factory-built components to achieve a custom look. ▶▶▶

Face-frame cabinets can accommodate a number of different door styles, but in general, convey a traditional appearance.

PRO TIP

Your site drawings should record how much the walls are out of plumb so that you can plan adequate scribe allowances into your cabinets.

Face-Frame or Frameless?

Depending upon your shop's capabilities, your personal skill level, and your project's needs, you may select between the two main carcase construction methods, face-frame or frameless. Both types have advantages and drawbacks.

Face-frame cabinets impart a more traditional appearance, especially when coupled with raised-panel doors, but of course, you can choose slab, flat-panel, or glass-insert doors, too. Typically, you'll use plywood for much of the carcase, but you'll craft the face frame itself, plus the doors and drawer fronts, from solid stock, and that raises a potential drawback. Working with solid wood requires a considerable investment simply in surfacing tools: a jointer, thickness planer, and probably an assortment of sanders. Making raised-panel doors adds a table-mounted router and a set of bits. Solid wood also requires a multistep finishing program.

Although that list may sound discouraging, the traditional appearance of face-frame styles often trumps it, especially when your goal is cre-

ating a built-in that looks original to the room design. Far more houses feature traditional styling than modern, and face-frame cabinets look more at home in them. Besides, you can sidestep many difficulties by purchasing some of the components ready-made, such as raised-panel doors, or by buying completed cabinets.

Frameless cabinets usually impart a sleek look, make efficient use of internal volume, and if surfaced with laminate (as this style often is), you don't have to finish them. In addition, the tools required are remarkably modest: a drill, some clamps, basic hand tools, and a tablesaw (although you could get by with a circular saw and cutting guide). If you want to make your own laminate-covered panels, you'll need a router or laminate trimmer. For more information on working with laminates, see "Countertops" on p. 108).

When frameless cabinets initially debuted in the United States a few decades ago, some people were turned off by a style that was so starkly

Frameless cabinets bring clean uncluttered lines to your design and impart a sense of the modern to your built-in.

minimalist it seemed institutional. Since then, however, two trends have made frameless cabinets more popular. First, consumers have increasingly embraced the "industrial" look. As an undeniable sign of this trend, consider the widespread popularity of commercial stainless steel appliances in today's kitchens. Second, frameless cabinets have developed more personality by using materials besides laminate—raised-panel doors teamed with a frameless carcase, for example.

Buying semi-custom cabinets is a great alternative to building the components from scratch.

Uniting Your Construction Strategy with the Installation Plan

After you've settled on an overall design for your project, you need to make some further choices, and they'll bring you another step closer to transforming your idea into reality. Two of these decisions, construction strategy and the installation plan, are intertwined. Here, you have three basic options: Install purchased cabinets, build in place, or build in shop and install at site

Let's take a brief look at each method so you can become familiar with the possibilities.

A continuous wood pull transforms a factory-made door into a custom-look original.

Install purchased cabinets

Purchasing factory-made cabinets doesn't require any cabinetmaking skills or construction time and bypasses the need for a workshop. It may, however, require waiting a few weeks for order processing and delivery. Kitchen stores and home centers feature displays so you can choose from a wide range of materials, styles, and configurations. Although you'll be faced with a number of choices, that number is finite, so these cabinets are sometimes called semi-custom or "manufactured to order." These terms distinguish such cabinets from those in a "custom" line, where

you can order virtually anything you want. Many retailers also offer low-cost or reasonably priced design assistance to help you select the style and configuration that will meet your needs.

Manufacturers usually produce both upper and lower cabinets in widths of 3-in. increments, so you'll never need to deal with a filler strip wider than that, a feature that helps you achieve a nearly custom appearance at a fraction of the cost. In addition, some manufacturers allow you to choose a custom cabinet depth in 1-in. increments. For example, to work within the limitations of the installation site, you can order upper cabinets only 10 in. deep instead of the usual

You may plan your installation so you can successfully scribe the cabinet so perfectly against the wall it won't even need a dab of painter's caulk between the stile and the wall. But even the best plans can turn sour. Always take filler strips and molding so you're prepared for the worst turn of events.

Factory-made cabinets are increasingly available in widths of 3-in. increments, a feature that minimizes the width of any filler strips you'll need at the end of a run

12 in. The cabinets arrive with a durable factory-applied finish, so you can skip that work as well. Manufacturers also provide prefinished filler strips and moldings to complete the project.

In addition to "ordered" cabinets, some of the big home centers carry a limited number of styles in stock, and you may also find a secondary stock line, consisting of unfinished cabinets.

Most home centers sell each frameless cabinet in two cartons—the carcase in one and the doors in the other. Although their motivation may be to simplify their inventory, separate packaging also maximizes your choices. You can customize components in several ways, such as cutting away the melamine banding of the doors and drawers and adding solid wood edging. Or you can purchase only the carcases and craft your own doors and drawer fronts.

Build in place

Years ago, the finish carpenter was often responsible for crafting kitchen and bath cabinets, as well as other built-ins, right at the job site. The cabinets were generally sturdy and serviceable but somewhat short on style. Today's homeowner, though, demands built-ins that look as sophisticated as fine furniture, and that virtually dictates building them in a shop setting. As a result, you're faced with two unattractive alternatives. You need to either move your shop to the installation site or constantly shuttle between your shop and the site, installing a few parts at a time.

Sometimes circumstances will force you to build in place, but it's never my first choice. The few times I've had to do it were frustrating because it was such an inefficient way to work. The only positive aspect was that I got plenty of exercise carrying things to and from the shop.

Another drawback is that if you—or a subsequent owner of your house—wants to relo-

cate the built-in, you're faced with a difficult or maybe impossible proposition. The assembly may not fit the doorway, leaving little to salvage because on-site cabinet removal proceeds in the same fashion as on-site installation: a few pieces at a time.

Build in shop, install at site

Just as sports teams enjoy an advantage when playing at home, you'll find building cabinets in your shop offers the best odds for success. You control the conditions in your shop, and that allows you to focus on the job at hand. Finishing is also best accomplished in your shop, because finishes are sensitive to dust, heat, and humidity—conditions you can adjust far more effectively in your shop than at the installation site.

Building cabinets in your shop, however, may require some strategic planning, depending on what style you choose. Face-frame cabinets take up a lot of room as you assemble them, so you'll need a storage area for them where they won't be damaged. Unless you have a huge shop, you'll want to get the cabinets out of there so you can continue building.

Frameless units, on the other hand, offer an advantage—knock-down construction makes the pieces portable so you don't need to assemble the cabinets as you make them. You can stack the finished components, haul them to the job site, and assemble and install them there. This makes transporting frameless cabinets much easier than face-frame units. With knock-down construction, you may be to able haul a wall of cabinets in a compact car—with nothing sticking out of the windows or strapped to the roof. Face-frame cabinets may require a big truck and a beefy helper.

Building a Face-Frame Cabinet

There are many different approaches to face-frame-cabinet construction. Some craftsmen advocate building the carcase first, but that involves so many calculations you run a significant risk something can go wrong. I prefer building the face-frame first to avoid those problems, and I use the frame to help me square the carcase.

Generally speaking, to minimize alignment problems and to economize on materials, divide a big project into the fewest number of modules. For example, build one four-door wall cabinet instead of a pair of two-door cabinets.

However, you also want to make certain that the components don't get so large they pose transportation problems. Above all, make absolutely sure you can get the completed cabinets to the installation site. Double-check your drawings for accuracy, then write a cutting list for the face-frame pieces, grouping all identical lengths together. Make columns listing both rough and finished dimensions.

Making the frame

1. Check your stock to make sure all pieces are identical in thickness, as shown in Photo **A**. If they aren't, thickness-plane all of the lumber into uniformity.

2. Rip stock for the rails and stiles ⅛ in. wider than their finished dimension, as shown in Photo **B**. The edge against the fence must be straight, but it doesn't need to be jointed before you make the cut.

3. With a miter saw, crosscut the blanks (unassembled face-frame members) 2 in. longer than their finished length, as Photo **C** shows. Of course, be sure to cut a few spares in case some pieces get damaged in subsequent machining steps.

WHAT CAN GO WRONG

Building a cabinet that's too big to get out of your shop or into an installation site may sound like the setup to a joke, but it's definitely not funny if it happens to you. Follow this rule of thumb and the laugh will never be on you: The maximum size for a section of cabinet carcase should be 24 in. by 36 in. by 72 in. You can put a cabinet this size on end onto a four-wheel furniture dolly and wheel it down narrow corridors and through all but the slimmest of doorways.

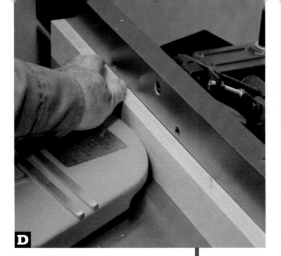

D

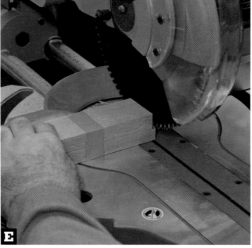

E

F

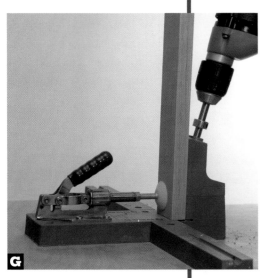

G

H

I

PROTIP

Call them by their
correct names: Horizontal
face-frame pieces are
rails; full-length vertical
pieces are stiles; shorter
vertical members are
intermediate rails or
mullions.

4. Joint one edge of each blank, as shown in Photo **D**, and stack the pieces with the unfinished edges facing the same direction. If you own a planer, you can plane these edges in batches to maintain identical widths. Absent a thickness planer, you'll need to joint the cut edge. Be sure you make the same number of jointing passes on each blank to get a uniform width.

5. Cut the blanks to finished length with your mitersaw. Use a stopblock setup or tape blanks into bundles, as shown in Photo **E**.

6. Lay out the rails and stiles in their assembled position, and label them. Marking the back face, as shown in Photo **F**, means you won't need to erase the marks later.

7. With a corded drill, bore pocket holes into the ends of the rails and intermediate stiles, as shown in Photo **G**.

8. Clamp the parts tightly before driving the screws to maintain perfect alignment of the face. Work on a large flat surface so you don't introduce any twist into the face frame. Using gauge blocks, as shown in photo **H**, ensures consistent spacing of intermediate rails with a minimum of measurement.

9. Smooth the face-frame joints, as shown in Photo **I**, by sanding with 100- and 120-grit abrasive in a random-orbit sander. Finally, sand with the grain, using a sanding block.

Make the carcase components

Beginning cabinetmakers usually don't have much trouble making the face-frame, but they often get confused when it's time to cut the other cabinet components. Uncertainty over joinery makes the situation seem even more confusing. Fortunately, you can eliminate all of the uncertainty by using a simple system that relates virtually all of the measurements back to the face frame. The sidebar on p. 47 illustrates the construction of a face-frame cabinet and explains how the dimensions of the parts and the joinery relate to each other.

Of course, you'll need to exercise reasonable care in sizing the rabbets, grooves, and dadoes so you'll have a strong cabinet, but don't make these joints so tight that you need to force the pieces together. Don't rely on the nominal thickness of the plywood: Take actual measurements of the thickness of a sheet before you size the recesses.

Aim for a fit that lets the parts slide together easily but not so loosely that the joint rattles. The grooves, dadoes, and rabbets provide some mechanical strength, but their main purpose is to register the parts in position until the glue dries or you drive fasteners.

The following procedure illustrates the assembly of a typical wall cabinet, but you'll employ a similar procedure for making base cabinets. I'll point out some of the differences between the two types during the step-by-step sequence.

1. As shown in Photo **A** on p. 44, rip and crosscut the carcase sides to size from ½-in. plywood. On their top edge, identify the front edge and the surface that will face the inside of the cabinet (see "Mirror-Image Sides" on p. 45). If you're building a base cabinet with a toe kick, mark and jigsaw the notches.

TRADE SECRET

There's no need to apply glue to joints assembled with pocket-hole screws. The glue makes the parts slippery during assembly, and doesn't add significant strength.

Other Face-Frame Joints

OF COURSE, THERE ARE MANY WAYS OF assembling face frames, including lap joints, mortises and tenons, and other worked joints. But the function of a face-frame doesn't require fancy joinery designed for high strength.

I like pocket-hole joinery because it's fast, easy, and accurate. It's also very forgiving of mistakes. Simply back out the screws, reposition the part, and drive the screws again.

I've also made face-frames with dowels and biscuits, and both methods can give you great results. You'll have to pay careful attention when you work with complex frames, though, to ensure that you follow an assembly sequence that doesn't make any piece impossible to add. The basic procedure involves working outward from the center.

Dowels are an old standby of face-frame construction, and biscuits also make sturdy joints.

A

B

C

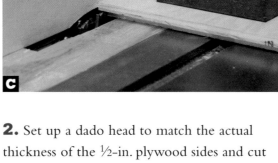

D

PRO TIP

Slicing solid lumber into cabinet components exposes fresh surfaces to the air, which can lead to moisture-content changes and cause warping, bowing, and twisting. Cutting can also release stresses contained within the structure of the wood, producing the same spectrum of problems. For those reasons, it's a good idea to move promptly from cutting to assembly. That will hopefully constrain the wood in the layout before it decides to move in a different direction.

2. Set up a dado head to match the actual thickness of the ½-in. plywood sides and cut a groove into the back side of the face-frame stiles ¼-in. deep and with its outer edge ¼-in. from each side, as shown in Photo **B**.

3. Attach a sacrificial face to your rip fence, and set the dado head to cut a rabbet ¼ in. wide. Set the cut depth equal to the actual thickness of your ¼-in. plywood. As shown in Photo **C**, run rabbets along the top and back inner edges of the sides. For base cabinets, omit the rabbet along the top edge.

4. Mark the location of the dado for the cabinet bottom. To do this, lay a side panel on the face-frame with their top ends flush and make a mark at the top edge of the bottom rail, as shown in Photo **D**.

5. Set your dado head for a cut whose width matches the actual thickness of your ¾-in. plywood and is ¼ in. deep. Position your rip fence so the top edge of the dado is at the mark you made on the side. I usually cheat about ¹⁄₃₂ in. lower than the mark, which positions the cabinet bottom a tiny bit below the top of the lower rail. This virtually eliminates the possibility that the edge of the bottom will be above the rail—a situation you'll want to avoid because it looks very nasty. Cut the dadoes into the inner faces of both sides, as shown in Photo **E**.

6. Insert a side into the groove in the face-frame so it's fully seated. Carefully measure from the back of the face-frame to the edge of the rabbet at the rear of the side, as shown in Photo **F**. This is the width of the bottom and the top. Rip these two parts to size.

E

F

G

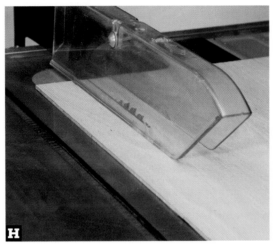

H

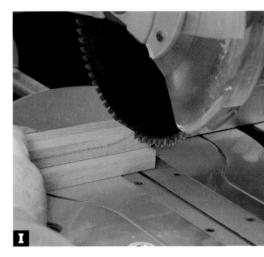

I

7. Measure the groove-to-groove distance on the face-frame, and add ½ in. to determine the length of the top and bottom. I find that a rigid rule gives a more accurate reading than a tape measure, so I use it when the scale of the project permits, as shown in Photo **G**. Cut the top and bottom to length.

8. Without changing the position of your rip fence, rip the back to width, as shown in Photo **H**. Crosscut the back to its finished size, equal to the length of the sides.

9. You can use a leftover piece of face-frame stock or a secondary wood for the hanging cleat. Rip lumber to make blanks for the top and bottom cleats. Square the end of each cleat, and mark the length, which is the groove-to-groove distance. Gang-cutting with a miter saw, as shown in Photo **I**, ensures identical lengths. Alternatively, you could use a stop-block setup.

Mirror-Image Sides

THE CARCASE SIDES OF A FACE-FRAME CABINET ARE MIRROR IMAGES of each other, not identical. Remembering this will prove particularly important if you drill shelf-pin holes or cut grooves for shelf standards before assembly. To eliminate confusion, set the sides next to each other with both interior faces upward, and use chalk to sketch the locations for dadoes, grooves, and other elements. Your chalk lines will help you eliminate mistakes.

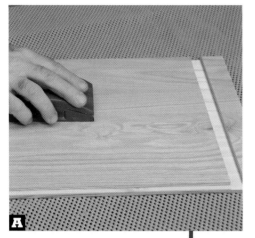

stricted access, as Photo  shows. If the outer surface of the sides will be visible after installation, sand them as well; 120-grit sandpaper is plenty.

2. Put the face-frame face down on a clean and flat assembly surface, and put a bead of glue into the two side grooves. Slip in the sides, as shown in Photo **B**, and make certain that they bottom out in the grooves.

3. Squirt glue into the dadoes that house the bottom. Also spread glue on the back edge of the face-frame that will mate with the front edge of the bottom. Slide the bottom into place, as shown in Photo **C**.

4. Lay down a bead of glue on the two surfaces where the bottom cleat touches the bottom and the face-frame. Make sure that the front edge of the bottom doesn't rise above the lower rail of the face frame, then secure the bottom cleat by driving a few brads, as shown in Photo **D**.

5. Glue the top cleat to the back top of the face frame. Before you drive the brads to secure it, make sure the ends of the cleats are flush with the groove in the face-frame and the

WHAT CAN GO WRONG

The actual thickness of plywood is always slightly less than its nominal dimension. Grooves and dadoes that accept plywood should be cut to match its measured thickness, not the nominal dimension.

Assemble the cabinet

Now you're nearly ready to assemble the cabinet. But before you start spreading glue, make sure you have all your supplies and tools organized. You'll need clean-up supplies ready to handle glue squeezeout, and clamps, cauls, deadblow mallet, and fasteners within easy reach.

Recruit a helper, if possible, so you can complete the assembly before the glue starts to set, and make sure you're working on a flat surface so your cabinet won't twist or rack.

1. If you want to drill holes for shelf pins or cut grooves for shelf standards, now is the time to do it (see "Drilling Side-Panel Holes" on p. 51). Sand the inside surfaces of the sides and back before assembly, while you still have unre-

Anatomy of a Face-Frame Carcase

THE SIZE OF THE FACE-FRAME AND the position of the grooves in its back govern virtually all other cabinet dimensions:

Face frame: ¾-in. solid stock.

Sides: ½-in. plywood; width is the finished depth of cabinet minus ½ in.; length equals the height of the face frame.

Back: ¼-in. plywood; width is the groove-to-groove dimension plus ½ in.; length equals the height of the face frame.

Bottom: ¾-in. plywood. To determine the width, put the sides into the grooves in the face frame, making sure they are fully seated. Measure from the back of the face-frame to the edge of the rabbet at the rear of the side. Length equals the groove-to-groove dimension plus ½ in.

Top and bottom cleats: Solid wood, ¾ in. by ¾ in. ; length equals the groove-to-groove dimension.

Hanging cleat: Solid wood, ¾ in. by 2 in.; length equals the groove-to-groove dimension.

Top (for upper cabinets only): ¼-in. plywood. Length and width are identical to bottom.

You've probably noticed that many of the parts share the same dimensions:

The top, bottom, and hanging cleats are all the same length.

Except for thickness, the top and bottom are the same size.

The width of the back equals the length of the top and bottom.

The sides and back are identical in length.

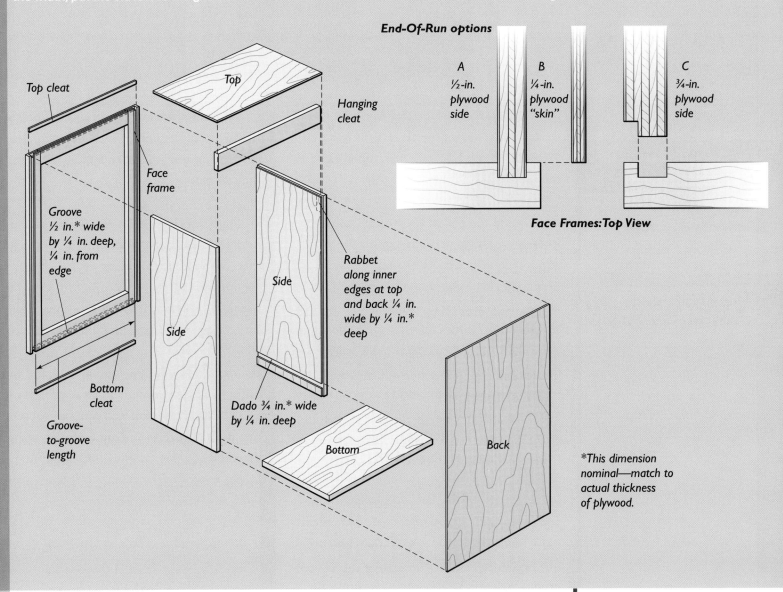

Top cleat

Top

Hanging cleat

Face frame

Groove ½ in.* wide by ¼ in. deep, ¼ in. from edge

Side

Side

Rabbet along inner edges at top and back ¼ in. wide by ¼ in.* deep

Bottom cleat

Groove-to-groove length

Dado ¾ in.* wide by ¼ in. deep

Bottom

Back

End-Of-Run options

A
½-in. plywood side

B
¼-in. plywood "skin"

C
¾-in. plywood side

Face Frames: Top View

*This dimension nominal—match to actual thickness of plywood.

E

F

G

rabbet at the top of the sides. Also make sure that the top edge of the cleat runs straight, as shown in Photo **E**. For a base cabinet, omit the top brace.

6. Position the end of the hanging cleat so its edges are flush with the rabbets at the top and rear of the sides. As you can see in Photo **F**, clamp the sides to hold the cleat while you drill pilot holes and drive a pair of #8 by 1½-in. screws through each side and into the cleat. If the side of the cabinet will be visible after installation, attach the hanging cleat with pockethole screws inside the carcase.

7. Before you put the back into place, mark the centerline of the bottom on the back edge of the sides so you'll know where to drive the fasteners. Put the back in place with its end flush with the top of the sides. Pneumatic staples are the cabinetmaker's usual fastener for this job, as Photo **G** indicates, but brads or flat-head screws would also work. Drive fasteners

into the sides, hanging cleat, and the bottom. If you use glue, apply it very sparingly because any squeezeout will make a huge mess inside the cabinet.

8. Stand up the cabinet and place cauls, if necessary, along the face frame to spread pressure and prevent damage from the clamps. Use clamps to draw the sides firmly into the face frame, as shown in Photo **H**, but make sure that the assembly remains flat on the table.

9. Spread glue before you drop the top into position, and then staple it. The top helps square up the cabinet, so you may need to back off the clamps slightly to fit the top, and then re-tighten them. Check the assembly with a framing square to ensure the cabinet is square, as shown in Photo **I**, then let the glue set.

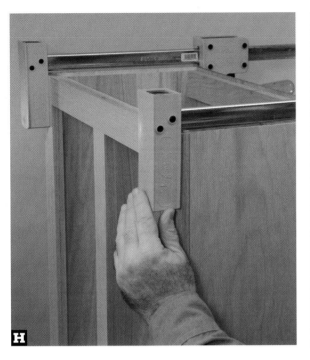

Frameless Cabinets

Cabinet factories lay down acres of melamine-covered surfaces every day, and such factory-made cabinets can save you a tremendous amount of time and effort. If you're satisfied with the stock-cabinet choices in the big-box store, you're ready to move ahead to assembly and installation.

If you want to customize the cabinet, you can use the components as the starting point for your own creative touches. For example, you can modify the doors and drawer fronts by adding a continuous pull molding along an edge. Or you can craft your own doors and drawer fronts from scratch. Cabinet distributors usually sell the doors separately from the carcases, so you're not forced to purchase doors and then discard them if you take the custom route. See "Doors" on p. 68 for details on making your own from solid stock or edge-banded plywood. "Countertops" on p. 108 shows you how to make components working with laminate. You can customize the front edges

of the carcase with iron-on veneer, solid wood facing, or laminate.

Factory-made frameless cabinetry typically employs knock-down hardware to speed assembly. If you make your own frameless carcase, you can also use these fasteners or choose alternative joinery, such as dowels, biscuits, or screws.

Assembling a manufactured frameless cabinet

The sequence on these pages demonstrates the assembly of a purchased cabinet, but following that we'll take a look at a jig system that allows you to quickly and accurately make your own frameless carcase with a minimum of equipment.

1. Lay out the components and inspect them for damage. Screw the hinge baseplates to the side of the cabinet, ensuring that they point in the correct direction, as shown in Photo **A** on p. 50. If you're uncertain about the direction, inspect the hinge arm to ensure that it will clip

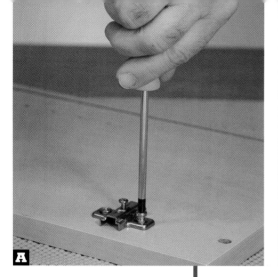

A

B

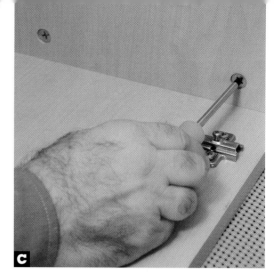

C

D

E

PRO TIP

A caul is a board that distributes clamping pressure, helping to achieve a secure bond along a joint with a minimum number of clamps.

WHAT CAN GO WRONG

Before clamping, slide your hand over the face-frame and caul to ensure that neither surface has grit on it. Any trapped material can dent the wood.

onto the baseplate with the cup on the outside of the cabinet.

2. Press the assembly hardware into the panels, making sure each fastener bottoms out in its holes, as shown in Photo **B**. The cams go into the top and bottom panels, with the arrow on the hardware pointing to the holes on the end of the panel. Press the cam bolts into the side panels—you shouldn't need more than finger pressure. The dowels are mainly used for positioning, so glue isn't mandatory.

3. Lower the top and bottom panels into position on one of the sides, making certain that the finished edges face the front. Use a manual screwdriver to lock the cams to the cam bolts

by twisting one-half turn clockwise, as shown in Photo **C**.

4. Position the hanging rails with the partially drilled starter holes facing the outside back of the cabinet, and assemble the second side in place, as shown in Photo **D**. Tighten the cams to secure this side.

5. Slide the back into the grooves and check for square by measuring for equal diagonals, as shown in Photo **E**. Tap nails through the starter holes to lock the back into place. Check again for square. The carcase is now ready for installation, and you'll add the doors and drawers after that step.

Frameless cabinets: Make your own

Building your own frameless cabinet carcases doesn't require nearly as many tools as face-frame construction. By using a jig, for example, you don't even need a drill press to create components with accuracy rivaling that of factory-made units. Before you begin, however, you'll find it helpful to become familiar with the European system.

Understanding the Euro system

The European system of making frameless cabinets is based upon a few rules that are logical and easy to understand. Once you understand them, you can tweak them to suit your needs.

Referring to the drawing at right, you can see that there are two types of holes in the end panels—construction holes and system holes. The construction holes, typically 8 mm in diameter, accept dowels that hold the carcase together. Centering the dowels in the thickness of the top and bottom panels means that the centerline of the construction holes is one-half the stock thickness from the end of the panel. Of course, you can substitute knock-down fasteners or biscuits for hidden joints, or even use screws if the ends of your cabinet won't be visible.

The vertical columns of holes, typically 5 mm in diameter, are called system holes because they accept system components such as hinge baseplates, shelf pins, or drawer runners. These holes are spaced 32 mm apart, a dimension that's sometimes used to name this method of cabinet construction: the 32-mm system. The centerline of each column of system holes is 37 mm from the cabinet's edge.

The system requires that the end panel's length (height) is equal to the stock thickness plus some multiple of 32 mm. For example, a close equivalent to a 24-in. wall cabinet would have 23 spacings at 32 mm each, plus the thickness of 16-mm stock—a total height of 752 mm.

To again strictly follow the system's logic, the cabinet's depth would be the sum of 74 mm (the two 37-mm offsets at the front and back of the cabinet) plus some multiple of 32 mm. Using 7 spacings of 32 mm plus 74 mm gives a total depth of 298 mm, which is very close to the standard 12-in. depth of face-frame cabinets.

Before you start bending these rules, you need to consider the symmetry this system creates. As long as both long edges are edge-banded, you can rotate or flip the side panels—this is called a balanced panel because it's symmetrical along two axes. A balanced panel eliminates fumbling or head-scratching during assembly because the panel is the same up or down and front to back. In our demonstration, we'll edge-band only the

DRILLING SIDE-PANEL HOLES

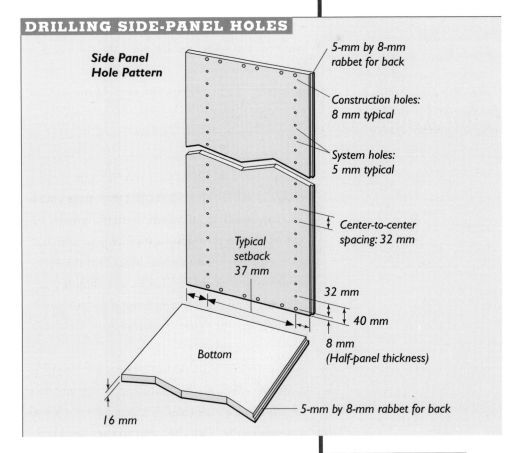

Side Panel Hole Pattern

5-mm by 8-mm rabbet for back

Construction holes: 8 mm typical

System holes: 5 mm typical

Center-to-center spacing: 32 mm

Typical setback 37 mm

32 mm

40 mm

8 mm (Half-panel thickness)

Bottom

5-mm by 8-mm rabbet for back

16 mm

A

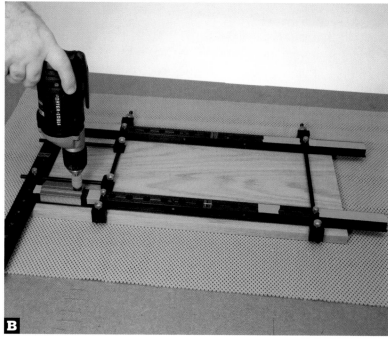

B

PROTIP

Always put cabinets together on a flat surface so you don't introduce any twist into the completed assembly.

front edge, which will convert the sides into half-balanced panels—the sides are identical but are assembled as mirror images of each other.

As long as you think through the full process, you can take some liberties with the rules to create custom panels. For example, you can drill system holes only where you need them instead of mindlessly boring full lines, which would place a potential shelf extremely close to the top or bottom of a cabinet.

Constructing a frameless carcase

A cabinetmaking jig system, such as the Lee Valley® model shown here, enables you to make your own frameless cabinets using only a table-saw, electric drill, a few clamps, and some basic hand tools. The jig's design ensures extraordinary consistency when drilling components for carcase components.

1. Apply edgebanding to blanks for your cabinet's components (see p. 57), and lay on a finish, if needed. Cut blanks for the cabinet sides and top/bottom to the finished width and length, as shown in Photo **A**. Set the tops and bottoms aside for now.

2. Assemble the jig, adjust its position according to its instructions, and clamp it to a side panel. (Longer rods adapt the jig to wider panels.) With a 5-mm bit equipped with a stop collar, drill the system holes in the face of the panel, as shown in Photo **B**. The bushing fits into the holes while the carrier straddles the rail. This ensures consistent spacing as you hop the carrier along the rail to create the line of holes. Masking tape covers holes in the rail you won't drill to eliminate wasted time and energy. If you need to drill holes on panels longer than the reach of the rails, refer to the jig's directions.

3. Change to an 8-mm bit with a stop collar, and swap the bushing in the carrier to match. Drill the line of construction holes along the rail at the top edge of the panel, as shown in Photo **C**. Rotate the jig to the opposite end of

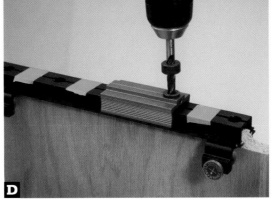

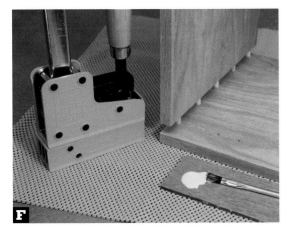

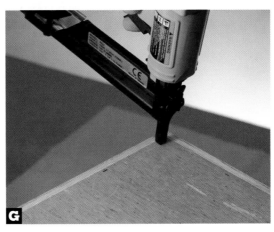

the panel to drill the construction holes for the bottom. If you're doing a big batch of cabinets, you'll work more efficiently if you purchase a second bushing carrier and utilize a separate drill for each bit size. Otherwise, drill the system holes in all the panels before changing the bushing and bit.

4. After you've drilled the system and construction holes in all the sides, convert one rail into a doweling jig by following the system's instructions. Check the accuracy of the jig's setup on a piece of scrap, then drill the construction holes into the ends of the top and bottom panels, as shown in Photo **D**.

5. Attach a sacrificial face to your tablesaw's rip fence and set it to cut the rabbet for the cabinet's back panel. The width of the rabbet is equal to the back's thickness, and the depth is one-half of the carcase panels' thickness. Referring to Photo **E**, cut the rabbet along the inner back edge of the sides, tops, and bottoms.

6. Carefully check the depth of your construction holes and cut your assembly dowels ⅛-in. shorter than double the depth of the holes. That will ensure that the dowels don't bottom out before the joint closes. Apply glue to the dowels, then assemble and clamp the joints, as shown in Photo **F**.

7. Cut the back and insert it into the rabbeted opening at the rear of the carcase. Narrow-crown staples, as shown in Photo **G**, are the fastener of choice, but you could substitute brads or flathead screws.

WHAT CAN GO WRONG

If the carcase components won't come together under moderate clamping pressure, the dowel joint may be suffering from hydraulic lock. This condition occurs when a tight-fitting dowel acts like a piston, creating high pressure as it compresses glue in the hole. If this happens, wait 30 seconds for the pressure to find an escape route, then try again. Repeat this operation a couple of times, if necessary. In extreme cases, you may need to disassemble the joint. To avoid the problem completely use dowels with flutes or spiral grooves that provide a relief path for trapped air and glue.

SHELVES

S helves form a vital part of many built-ins and range from a glass shelf holding a featherweight collectible to a torsion box capable of supporting an anvil. In this chapter, we'll explore how to choose shelf material that's appropriate to its supporting role, as well as how to add aprons and other reinforcements that boost a shelf's strength.

We'll also review some easy-to-understand rules of thumb for shelving design. These guidelines will help you see how changes in a shelf's dimensions affect its resistance to sagging under a load. That way, you can avoid shelving snafus or confidently fix them.

Of course, the shelves themselves are only part of the story—you'll also need to choose and install a support system. We'll sort through the various choices, including pins, pilasters, and brackets, reviewing their relative strengths and shortcomings. You'll see proven solutions that work great and look good, too. ▶ ▶ ▶

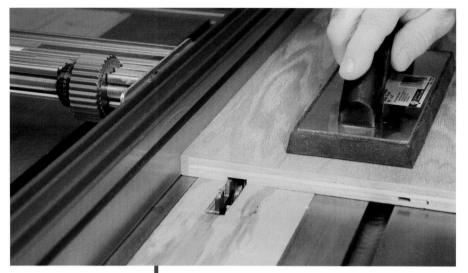

To install shelf standards, use a dado head in your table saw to cut grooves into the cabinet sides.

A

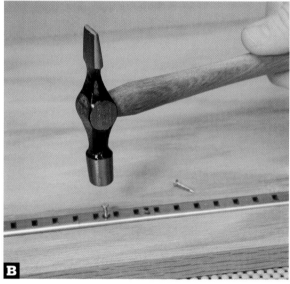

B

PRO TIP

Two strategies for moving assembled cabinets: Remove the shelves (and write their position on the back edge), or use clips that lock the shelves into position and move the entire cabinet with the shelving in place.

Supporting Cabinet Shelves

You'll find two predominant systems for supporting shelves in cabinets: metal standards with clips and shelf pins in holes drilled in the sides. For strength, it's no contest—the clear winner is the metal standard (sometimes called a pilaster). The metal won't bend in virtually any reasonable circumstance—and even in some unreasonable situations. In addition, the standards efficiently transfer the load to the bottom of the cabinet.

Pins, especially the plastic ones, can sag or even snap, and heavy weights on any pins can cause transform the holes into ovals. But even with all their shortcomings, pins often prevail for aesthetic reasons. You'll find pins in a wide range of diameters, from a tiny 5 mm to a robust $3/8$ in. The larger the pin diameter, the greater its strength, and the less likely it is to deform the hole. Pin sleeves add a modicum of strength, but their real benefit is hiding tearout at the hole.

Install metal shelf standards

When cutting dadoes for standards, I cut the grooves for a relatively snug fit edge to edge, but set the depth so the front of the standard is about $1/16$ in. above the surface of the wood. This keeps the ends of shelves from scraping the inner sides of the carcase when you install them.

1. Temporarily screwing the standard to a scrap board, as shown in Photo **A**, keeps the metal from twisting when you cut it. Always hacksaw the top end of shelf standards (not the bottom end) to the length you need. That way, the clip slots on all the standards will lie on the same plane, ensuring that each shelf will rest solidly on all four clips.

2. Drive the nails (they're packed with the shelf clips) to secure the standards to the carcase, as shown in Photo **B**. Make sure that the nails are not too long for the thickness of your sides.

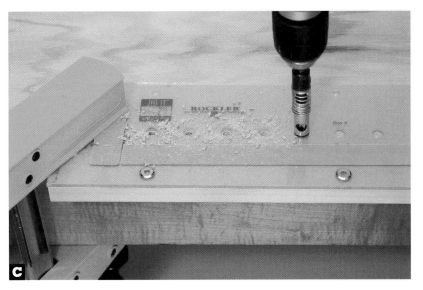

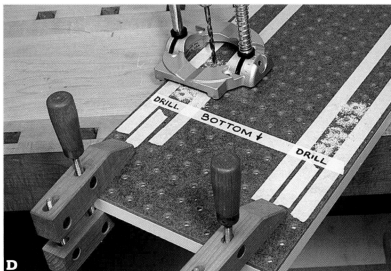

Drill shelf-pin holes

1. With a commercial shelf-pin drilling jig, as shown in Photo **C**, you can use a spring-loaded bit that registers into the jig's holes for accuracy and takes the worry out of drilling too deeply.

2. If you don't own a commercial jig, use perforated hardboard—it's an old standby of shop-made jigs, as shown in Photo **D**. This relatively soft material dooms the jig to a relatively short lifespan, but it's so inexpensive and quick to make that the sacrifice isn't painful. Use a stop on your drill bit, and be careful to drill perpendicular to the panel. A portable drill guide ensures perpendicularity and consistent depth.

With either a commercial or homemade jig, cover unwanted openings with tape to prevent stray holes.

Shelving Materials and Edging

The harsh realities of economics dictate that solid-wood shelves are a rarity. There is, however, a practical alternative. Manufactured panels dominate the field of shelf materials, and you'll narrow down your choices based on appearance, price, function, and strength (see "Plywood" on p. 22 and "Other Sheet Goods" on p. 26 for more information about the relative merits of various panels). The sidebar "Rules of Thumb for Shelving Design" on p. 59 also gives some strength-related advice.

• You'll also have to decide how you want to edge your shelving. In some cases, you may be able to use self-edged melamine shelving (self-edged means that the same material covers the edges as its faces), but you can also use melamine edge tape with a heat-activated adhesive. Simply iron it on, as shown in Photo **A**, on p. 58. To skip the ironing, you can purchase melamine and wood veneer edgebanding that has a backing of pressure-sensitive adhesive (PSA).

WHAT CAN GO WRONG

If you forget to drill the holes for shelf pins before gluing up the cabinet, don't worry. Simply slide a shelf-drilling jig inside the cabinet, registering it against the bottom of the cabinet to ensure uniform heights for no-rock shelves. In fact, this system is so fast, easy, and accurate that some cabinetmakers use it exclusively, instead of drilling the sides before assembly.

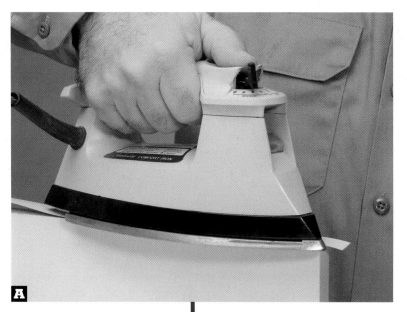

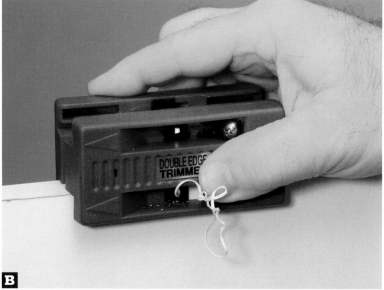

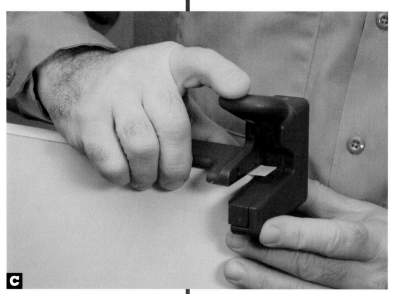

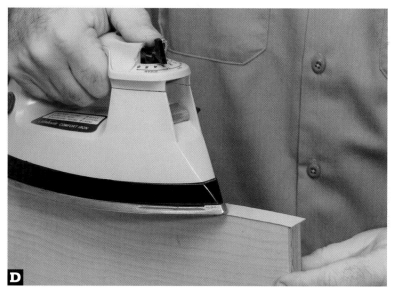

PROTIP

Prefinish wood shelf edging before attaching it to melamine or laminate panels. This eliminates the need for tedious masking.

• A banding trimmer, as shown in Photo **B**, quickly slices away excess melamine for a neatly finished edge. Look for the arrow on the tool that indicates the direction of its work.

• An end trimmer, shown in Photo **C**, squarely snips the end of the tape.

• Iron-on veneer made from real wood, seen in Photo **D**, goes on the same way as melamine, but you'll need to mind the grain direction during trimming to avoid tearout. You won't be able to trim both sides at once as you do with grainless melamine, so use only one half of the side trimmer (or a block plane) to remove overhanging veneer.

Rules of Thumb for Shelving Design

MANAGING THE PHYSICAL PROPERTIES OF SHELVING becomes easier when you apply a few basic principles to their design.

• Increasing the length of a shelf by a factor divides its total load-carrying ability by that same factor. (This assumes that width and all other conditions, such as species and thickness, remain constant.) For example, if you double the length of a shelf, it can carry only the half the weight. The corollary is also true: Making a shelf half as long doubles its load-carrying capacity.

• Increasing the thickness of a shelf by a factor increases its load rating by the cube of that factor. (Again, this assumes that width and all other factors remain constant.) For example, doubling the thickness increases its rating by the cube of 2 (2 x 2 x 2 = 8). Of course, the corollary of this rule is also true. For example, a shelf that's one-half as thick can handle only one-eighth of the weight. You get an even more dramatic result by tripling the thickness of a shelf because it cubes 3 as a factor (3 x 3 x 3 = 27). It may sound incredible, but tripling the thickness of shelf makes it 27 times stronger.

• Even when load-bearing capacity is not a major design issue, limit shelf length to 36 in. or less whenever possible. This also makes sense when you consider the economy of materials, because you can get three shelves about 32 in. long from one length of plywood.

• Don't make shelves deeper than necessary. For example, 9 in. is adequate for most hardcover books.

• If a shelf is 18 in. or deeper, such as in a base cabinet, consider a sliding tray, pull-out baskets, or other strategies that provide easy access to items in the back.

Ranging from weak to wonderful, this selection of shelves hints at some of the design choices that can boost load-carry capacity. From top: MDF, melamine-covered particleboard, edgebanded plywood, solid pine shelf, plywood with an apron on the front only, and a plywood shelf with aprons front and rear.

Attempting to cut
shelves and banding or
aprons all to precisely
matching lengths is dif-
ficult enough in itself,
but trying to assemble
the components with
their ends perfectly flush
raises the difficulty level
even higher. Sidestep
those problems by ini-
tially cutting both the
shelves and the aprons or
banding into overlength
blanks. After joining the
parts, cut the assembly
to final size. It's an effortless way to get perfectly
flush ends.

• Tape provides enough clamping pressure for edging strips, as shown in Photo **E**. Refer to the procedure on door edging on p. 70 for more tips on cutting, applying, and trimming these strips. You can also add solid wood band-ing to plywood shelves using the matched pair of router bits shown on p. 153.

• In the metal section of most home centers and some hardware stores, you'll find aluminum trim channel in various widths, designed to fit the edge of plywood sheets, as shown in Photo **F**. For a shelf edge that will be visible, you can bring the metal up to a high shine, but the procedure involves a number of polishing compounds and a great deal of time. Instead, I like to finish the aluminum with 120-grit paper in a random-orbit sander. This process quickly obliterates imperfections and generates a pleas-ing finish that looks like a light coating of frost on the metal. Experiment with different sand-paper grits to discover the effect you like best.

This aluminum trim channel is usually a bit too wide for the thickness of hardwood-veneered plywood, but you can correct that situ-ation easily with a few taps of a deadblow mallet. Friction alone is sufficient to keep the edging in place, but adding a line of roundhead screws or other fasteners can give the shelf edge an indus-trial look. If possible, use aluminum fasteners to avoid the corrosive effect that can occur when you put dissimilar metals together.

• Another style of aluminum trim is the 1½-in.-wide T-molding shown in Photo **G**. (The name "T-molding" comes from its profile as viewed from the end.) The barbed projection fits snugly into a ⁵⁄₆₄-in. kerf cut by a router slot-cutting bit. You can purchase this trim in several styles and colors, and use it also as a fac-ing on the rails and stiles of a cabinet.

• Plastic T-molding that's ¾ in. wide is the right size to conceal raw plywood edges, as shown in Photo **H**, and it fits into a ¹⁄₁₆-in. kerf cut into the edge. For laminated sheet goods, choose the ¹³⁄₁₆-in. width, which requires a ⁵⁄₆₄-in. kerf.

Off on a Tangent

SOMETIMES, YOU CAN EASILY support a shelf on the ends, but the middle will sag. Instead of adding unsightly and bulky hardware, drill a hole into a stud so a steel rod inserted in the hole will lie tangent to the lower surface of the shelf. You'll boost the shelf's load capacity with-out sacrificing useful storage volume.

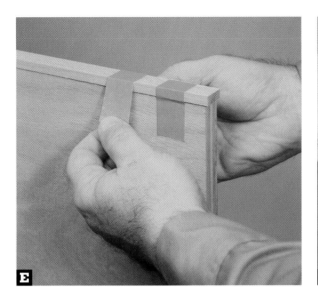

E

F

G

H

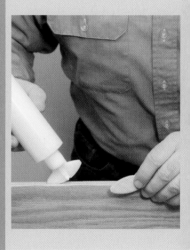

A plate groove is typically ¼ in. by ¼ in., with its rear edge 2 in. from the back of the shelf.

Making Strong Shelves

When you need to strengthen your shelves, you can rely on a number of techniques.

• Aprons are one of them. Pocket-hole screws, as shown in photo **A**, are a quick way to attach aprons, and glue isn't necessary. In fact, glue will make the parts slippery and assembly more difficult. If you object to the appearance of the pocket holes, simply glue and clamp the apron.

• A good glue bond between shelf and apron will probably provide all the strength you need, but a biscuit joint, as shown in photo **B**, offers additional advantages. First, the biscuits (housed in slots in the apron and the shelf's edge) help align the parts (but you'll still need to tweak their position during the clamp-up). Second, the biscuits provide additional glue surface and also supply a structural boost to the joint.

• To gain some strength while minimizing the metallic appearance of aluminum trim edge (see p. 61), put the channel on the back edge of the shelf.

• Give shelves a quantum leap in strength by adding a metal angle between the shelf bottom and the back edge of its apron, as shown in Photo **C**. Match the material of the screws to the metal of the angle. This prevents corrosion that can result from the contact of dissimilar metals.

More Shelving Choices

A pull-out tray maximizes accessibility to items in the back of a cabinet. Cabinets with inside corners are notorious space wasters, but you can

see p. 61

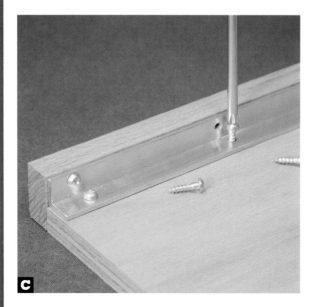

A

B

C

A pull-out tray is easy to build, and it glides the contents of deep shelves within easy reach.

solve that problem by installing a revolving shelf unit or large lazy-susan trays.

Wall shelves

Open shelving can add storage, convenience, and style to every room in your house. In many cases, open-shelf installation can provide almost instant gratification because you're not committed to a lengthy design process, and you certainly don't need a shop full of expensive machinery to install a few feet of shelves. If you're indecisive or afraid of commitment, take comfort in the fact that a simple open-shelf project also uninstalls quickly.

Shelving projects that are more permanent look like built-ins, not add-ons. One example is described in "Installing Standards and Panels" (p. 65). With short standards you can build storage into a small niche. Select long standards, and you can transform a blank wall into a floor-to-ceiling library within a weekend.

Angled shelf

The world isn't flat, and you're not limited to horizontal shelves. Consider an angled shelf with a lip on its front edge to display a favorite book or to keep a reference volume poised for easy

access. Another use: Display the current issue of a magazine, and stash back issues behind the shelf. The illustration "Angling a Shelf," below, shows how to pivot the shelf on a simple system of screw eyes and metal pins.

Making good shelves look great

The real focus of any shelving system should be the contents, not the shelving materials or construction. If you want truly picture-perfect

---

ANGLING A SHELF

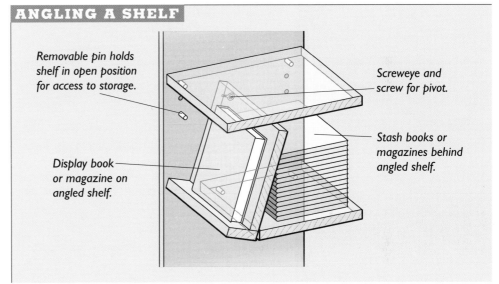

Removable pin holds shelf in open position for access to storage.

Screweye and screw for pivot.

Display book or magazine on angled shelf.

Stash books or magazines behind angled shelf.

Build a Torsion Box

A TORSION BOX IS A GREAT SOLUTION for long spans that must support substantial weight. One way of building a box is to utilize the same honeycomb paper product that door makers sandwich between veneers to make so-called hollow-core doors. Another way is to make a frame, then fill it with a gridwork made from strips of solid wood or plywood glued and stapled together. Glue a sheet of plywood to the top and bottom of the web to complete the structure. Spread waxed paper on your workbench so that you don't accidentally glue the box to the surface during assembly.

Pigeonholes make it easy for you to look more organized than you actually are. Make the unit as a separate piece so that you can swap it for a different size if technology or your needs change.

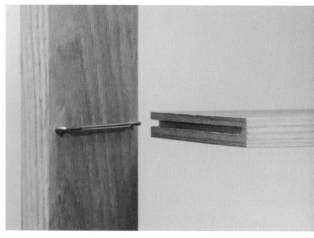

Invisible wire supports engage ⅛-in. holes in the cabinet's side, and slide into blind kerfs in the shelf's ends. The result is an invisible support system that can be repositioned.

WHAT CAN GO WRONG

When you need glass for a shelf or door, make a template from thin plywood or hardboard to prove the fit. Take the template to the glass shop to eliminate potential errors that can result from using different tape measures. This procedure saves time and prevents frayed nerves by defusing disputes.

results, consider hiring an interior designer to "stage" your shelves. Make a few telephone calls, and you may find that the cost of the service is not as extravagant as you might think.

With a little bit of time and thought, though, even people who don't believe they have designer genes can achieve outstanding results. The following tips will head you in the right direction.

• From a purely practical standpoint, you'll minimize shelf stress by putting heavy items on fixed shelves or as close to the shelf supports as possible. In addition to reducing the physical strain on the shelf, you'll simultaneously avoid a tense appearance.

• If part of the display includes books, distribute them among several shelves instead of grouping all of them together. Also vary their positions: some on edge, some stacked, some face-front, showing the cover.

• Introduce a variety of materials and textures to boost interest. Textiles, foliage, metal, glass, and other items have interest in themselves but they also create contrast. For example, a smooth ceramic vase looks even more lustrous in the company of textured stone bookends.

• Create a focal point for the display by drawing attention to an important item. Selecting a bright color—or merely one that contrasts with the overall tone of the other items—is an effective strategy.

• Create deliberate height variations instead of simply lining up items in descending height like a chorus line of dancers.

• As you fill the shelves, stand back every so often to survey your overall design.

Narrow shelves are easy to build and install, and provide a display venue for photographs, artwork, plates, and other collectibles. See the photo at right for installation instructions.

Pockethole screws can attach narrow light-duty shelves to wall studs. Install screws under the shelf if it's below eye level and above the shelf if it's above your viewpoint.

Installing Standards and Panels

SCREW STANDARDS WITH A DOUBLE ROW of slots into a stud wall, and you'll have a shelf system of superior strength. The standards, available in several colors, are about $5/8$ in., deep, but you can conceal most of that depth by installing $1/2$-in. plywood panels between them. Initially rip blanks for the strips about 16 in. wide, and apply the finish. You'll cut them to final width during installation. Work your way across the wall, alternating the installation of standards and strips. Apply construction adhesive to the back of the panel and you'll need only a couple of finishing nails to maintain their position until the adhesive sets.

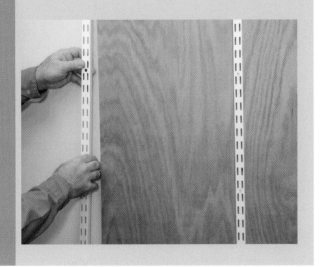

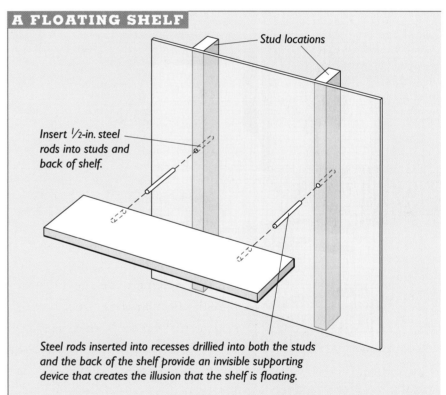

Stud locations

Insert $1/2$-in. steel rods into studs and back of shelf.

Steel rods inserted into recesses drilled into both the studs and the back of the shelf provide an invisible supporting device that creates the illusion that the shelf is floating.

SAFETY FIRST

If you're considering glass shelves for your project, get advice from your glass supplier early in the design phase. Make sure you understand the load limits of various glass thicknesses, and also discuss support strategies that avoid concentrated stresses. In addition to eliminating the risk of shattered shelving, you'll also protect the contents of the shelf.

DESIGN
OPTIONS

◁ **The range hood dictated a deeper cabinet above it, making it the perfect depth to display large dinner plates in an easily accessible divided rack.**

▲ **Open shelving makes access easy, and even more convenient here by dropping the upper cabinets down to virtually eliminate reaching. The lowered cabinets also expose the row of windows, bringing in additional sunlight.**

▶ Lazy Susans answer the question of what to do with the corner cabinet and let you find cooking supplies and condiments quickly. Install no-pole units on shelves so you can see all the contents at a glance.

▶ Put small spaces at the end of cabinet runs to work by adding pull-out shelves. Build your own or incorporate any number of commercial components into your design.

▲ Open cubbies are easy to build and help keep small things organized. Frame the space with a valance so you can hide low-voltage lighting.

DOORS

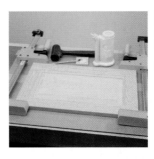

More than any other single element of a cabinet, doors set the style, so you'll want to choose wood species and construction methods consistent with your design theme.

Slab doors are relatively easy, even for a beginner. Raised-panel doors, though, seem to intimidate many serious hobbyists, and divided-light doors leave even some veterans with a glazed expression. But door making is not a mystical art; it's a specific sequence of procedures you can master. Of course, we can't discuss every method in a single chapter, but other resources can show you how to build a tambour (rolltop) door or make specialized joints.

On the other hand, farming out the door production saves you the expense of tooling up for the job, as well the time you'd need to make them. There's no shortage of mail-order suppliers, as well as local cabinet shops eager to accept the work. Get both the doors and false drawer fronts from the same supplier so the stock and style match throughout. ▶ ▶ ▶

Getting the Grain Right

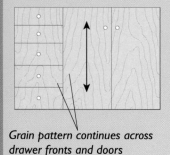
Slab Doors

Slab doors are easy to fabricate from hardwood plywood, melamine panels, or laminate-covered panels. But no matter what material you choose, you'll probably want to apply some type of banding to hide the raw edges of the panels.

When self-edging a laminate panel (applying laminate on the edges and ends), use the following sequence to help minimize the number of dark seams along the corners:

• Laminate the back of an oversized blank, and saw the blank to size.

• Cut laminate pieces wider than the thickness of the door and band and trim the top and bottom edges. Adhere the bandings with contact cement, then remove the excess with a flush-trimming bit in a laminate trimmer or router.

• Band and trim the side edges.

• Laminate and trim the door face.

For more details about applying laminate, see "Countertops" on p. 108.

Self-edging a melamine panel is simpler because the faces come with the melamine applied. See p. 57 for the tools and procedures you'll need for melamine banding, as well as for iron-on veneer made from real wood.

Another alternative is peel-and-stick wood veneer or melamine banding. When applying either of these self-sticking edgings, use a roller that puts plenty of pressure so you get a tight bond. Stain real-wood veneer strips lightly. Otherwise, solvents can migrate under the banding, attacking the adhesive and loosening its grip.

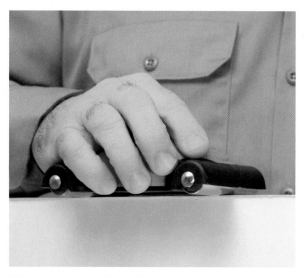

This tool has pairs of interchangeable rollers: The rubber ones provide moderate force but the steel set maximizes the pressure.

Apply hardwood banding

Hardwood banding strips make an excellent choice for edging plywood panels, in either a matching or contrasting species. Of course, you can also apply this banding to laminate panels.

The system I use for banding eliminates the tedious process of trying to cut the strips to precise measurements. You'll get perfect corners without squinting at layout lines.

1. Begin by slicing your banding strips, as shown in Photo **A**. Cutting them ¼ in. thick simplifies the math of sizing the door. Make the strips about ⅛ in. wider than the door's thickness. For safety and accuracy, install a zero-clearance throat plate (see "Zero-Clearance Tablesaw Insert" on p. 77) and use a feather-board and push block. Run the edge of your board over your jointer before the first and succeeding cuts to establish a good glue surface. Mark each sawn face with a pencil. You'll sand these faces after completing the door banding.

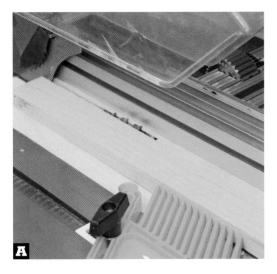

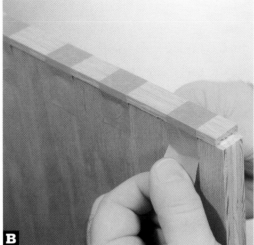

PROTIP

Even though your
flush-cutting bit will
produce a smooth edge,
sand the edges to final
smoothness, making sure
you keep them square. If
you want, you can rout
a roundover or chamfer
along the perimeter of
the door.

2. Cut your plywood door blank to its exact height, but 1 in. wider than its finished width. Then cut a pair of banding strips about ½ in. shorter than the blank's width and glue them centered on the top and bottom of the blank, as shown in Photo **B**. Use glue sparingly to minimize squeezeout. Masking tape supplies adequate clamping pressure.

3. Take your tall router table fence (see p. 97), and attach two strips of ¼-in. hardboard with double-faced tape. This creates clearance for the overhanging edges of the banding. Align the bearing of a flush-trim bit with the face of the hardboard. Trim both sides of the banding flush with the face of the panel, as shown in Photo **C**.

4. As shown in Photo **D**, cutting the panel to finished width by slicing ½ in. from each edge simultaneously cuts the banding to perfect length.

5. Glue and tape the banding on the sides of the door, overhanging each end at least ½ in. After the glue dries, trim the edges of the banding flush with the faces using your router-table setup. Then, with a flush-cut saw,. as shown in Photo **E**, cut the ends of the banding flush.

Making Door Frames

When planning door frames for your built-in, your first decision will center on the type of joinery you want to use. Then you'll need to calculate dimensions (see "Sizing the Stiles, Rails, and Panels" on p. 78).

Biscuits, dowels, and other joints

Biscuit joiners are relatively inexpensive, and you can use this tool to make strong joints in both carcases and doors. Clamp each piece down to a flat surface before you cut the slots to ensure that the assembled faces of the rails and stiles will be flush. But even with that precaution, the joint may have some play in it because the biscuit is slightly thinner than its slot, so you may want to apply a clamp across the face of each joint to ensure flush alignment.

A doweled joint can be quite strong, but even the best doweling jigs require you to work very carefully to get consistent results. If the jig tips even slightly while you're drilling—which is very easy when working on the ends of rails—the joint can be impossible to assemble.

A half-lap corner joint is extremely strong because of the enormous amount of long-grain-to-long-grain gluing area. It's also relatively easy to machine accurately. On the downside, every corner of the door shows some end grain at these joints. An end-grain surface invariably finishes darker than face and edge grain, so it can be visually distracting. You'll find that objection less troublesome, however, on inset doors.

Some people prefer pockethole joints as a strong and efficient way of building doors. As a personal matter, I'm a huge fan of pockethole joinery for face frames and other hidden structural applications, but not for door joints where the plugs would be visible when the door's open. But if you don't object to the plugs (of if you're painting the doors), get out the pockethole jig (see p. 42).

There's one kind of joint that's a mainstay of door construction, and that's the mortise and tenon. To make strong mortise-and-tenon joints, as well as most other joints, you have to be able to cut perfectly square corners.

see p. 42

You can machine half-lap joints with a single setup on your tablesaw.

A biscuit joint is strong, invisible, and easy to make.

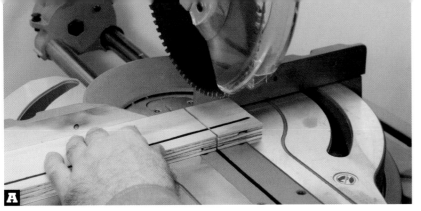

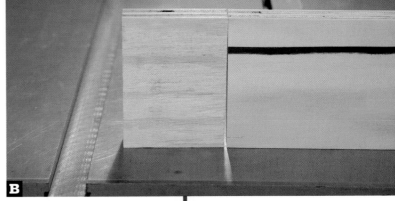

Perfectly square cuts

Virtually all door corner joints require perfectly square cuts. Even a slight misalignment can produce gaps or an out-of-square door. Many woodworkers endure needless frustration believing that accurate joints require pricey gauges and gizmos. In fact, you can set up for perfectly square cuts without even owning a square.

When you understand this procedure, you can accurately set your tablesaw or mitersaw: squaring the blade to the table, squaring the miter gauge to the blade, or setting your mitersaw for perfectly vertical cuts. Although the following sequence illustrates the procedure on a mitersaw, you can adapt it to squaring your tablesaw also.

1. Here's how to square your mitersaw's blade to the fence. Begin by ripping a piece of stock about 3 in. wide. The important thing here is that the sides are parallel. Draw a line on one face of the ripped stock near the edge. Lay the board on the saw with the marked edge up and near you, and cut a piece about 2 in. long, as shown in Photo **A**.

2. Take the pieces to a flat reference surface such as a tablesaw, and stand them on edge, inverting the cutoff so the marked line is at the top back. Lightly push the cutlines together, looking for a gap. If there's a space at the bottom, as in Photo **B**, you'll need to swing the blade to the right to eliminate it. An opening at the top, of course, means you'll move the blade to the left.

3. Make very slight adjustments because the gap doubles the angular error. Be patient and persistent until the two pieces align perfectly. Then the blade will then be exactly at 90 degrees to the fence. Set the cursor on the angle scale to zero, as shown in Photo **C**.

4. If you have a tilting mitersaw, set the blade at a right angle to the table by repeating the procedure with the wood placed vertically, as shown in Photo **D**. Again, zero out the tilt scale after you've achieved the right setting.

TRADE SECRET

Consistent stock
thickness simplifies door construction. Run the rail and stile stock through a thickness planer or sander to ensure uniformity.

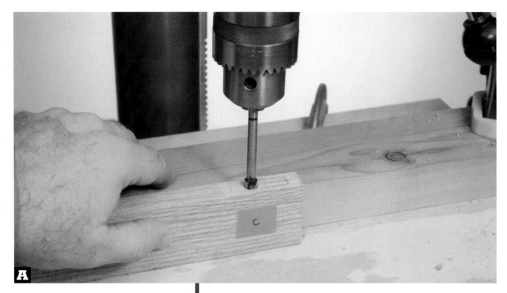

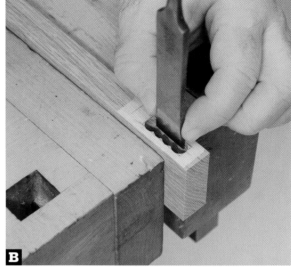

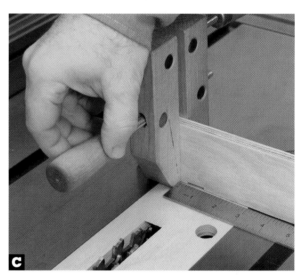

It's a good policy to make the cabinet carcase first so you can directly measure the opening each door will occupy. This can help eliminate some embarrassing mistakes. For example, if two overlay doors meet within a single opening in a face-frame cabinet, don't calculate an overlay at the middle. That would make the pair of doors too large for the space.

Mortise and tenon joint: Regular

The mortise and tenon is a strong joint that's a traditional favorite for doors and other structural applications. There are numerous variations, but we'll tackle a fairly simple version in ¾-in. by 2-in. stock.

1. Lay out a mortise ⅜ in. wide by 1¼ in. long by 1 in. deep along a centerline on the mortise stock. Using a ⅜-in. Forstner bit in your drill press, drill 1¹⁄₁₆-in. deep holes at each end of the layout, then drill overlapping holes along the centerline to excavate most of the waste, as shown in Photo **A**. Using a hollow chisel mortiser simplifies this process and also eliminates the hand-chiseling required in the next step.

2. With a chisel, pare the sides of the mortise smooth, as shown in Photo **B**, but be careful not to widen the opening. Square the ends of the mortise.

3. Set up a ¾-in.-wide stack dado set in your tablesaw, with the height at about ⅛ in. Attach an auxiliary face to your miter gauge, run it through the dado set, and clamp a stopblock

1 in. from the edge of the cut, as shown in Photo **C**.

4. Form the tenon's thickness with dado cuts on both sides, as demonstrated in Photo **D**. Raise the blade in tiny increments to sneak up on a perfect fit: one that slides easily into the recess of the mortise but without sloppiness.

5. After you've cut all the tenons to the correct thickness, set the rails on edge to remove the waste at the top and bottom of the tenons, as

shown in Photo **E**. Adjust the blade so that the tenon's width matches the mortise's length.

6. You may need a shoulder plane, rasp, or chisel to fine-tune the joints, as shown in Photo **F**. Be sure to remove equal amounts from both cheeks of the tenon to keep it centered in the mortise. When you're satisfied with the dry-fit of the joints, apply glue and clamp the assembly on a flat surface. Waxed paper prevents the glue from sticking the door to the table.

Mortise and tenon joint: Easy

Even when everything goes well with the regular method of making mortise and tenon joints, you'll probably have to rely on quite a bit of fussy hand work to get the joints to fit just right. The time may not be significant if you're making only a couple of doors, but if you get into a big project, it can multiply quickly.

That's why several manufacturers produce jigs designed to reduce the time, effort, and skill required to quickly produce mortise and tenon joints. The best jig I've used is the Leigh® FMT (Frame Mortise and Tenon). You'll invest an hour or so in the initial setup, but after that you'll crank out accurate and identical joints so fast you'll almost feel guilty. Even if you remove the router from the sub-base to do other work, you can restore it to perfect position in about one minute. The jig has micro-adjust capability, so you have full control over how snugly your joints fit. And even better than that, the adjustment knobs are calibrated so you can change bits and guides for a different joint size and then instantly restore your original settings. The Leigh jig is pricey, but if you value your time and want accuracy, you won't be disappointed.

TRADE SECRET

Always keep stop blocks elevated above the table surface so sawdust doesn't build up in the corner. The trapped waste would defeat the accuracy of your setup.

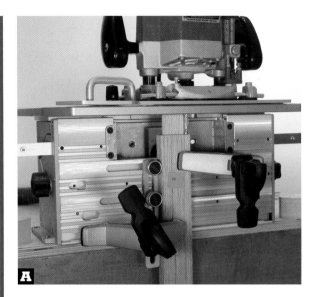

A

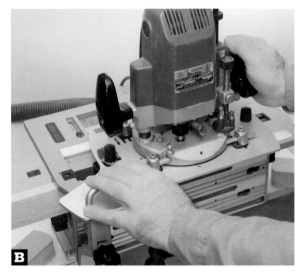

B

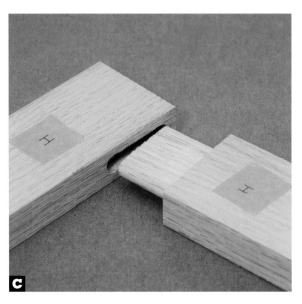

C

1. The jig comes with a thoroughly illustrated manual, so there's no need to detail the setup here. Cam clamps hold the rails vertically, as shown in Photo **A**, to rout the tenons. You make a light clockwise climb cut to cleanly sever the wood fibers, then guide the pin of the sub-base counterclockwise around the template to finish the tenon.

2. Clamp the stile horizontally, as shown in Photo **B**. Adjust the depth stop so that the mortise will be at least $1/16$ in. deeper than the tenon's length. Working from left to right, plunge the router to make a series of overlapping holes along the mortise's length. Lock the bit at its full depth, and slide the router left-right-left to finish forming the mortise.

3. As you can tell from Photo **C**, the joint is so well aligned on the face that it will hardly need sanding.

Stub mortise and tenon

The stub mortise and tenon produces a door with a square profile on the inner perimeter of the frame, making it suitable for a variety of styles, including Arts and Crafts, Shaker, and modern. The joint isn't as strong as a full mortise and tenon, but it's considerably easier to make. In addition, if your door will house either glass or a removable wood panel, this joint will give you a jump start on removing the waste from the rabbet. As a rule of thumb, the thickness of the tenon is about one-third of the stock's thickness.

A stack dado set in your tablesaw makes the joint. Here's a quick tip: when you're cutting the grooves, run each piece over the cutter twice, alternating the face that's set against the rip fence. This ensures that the groove will be centered in the width of each piece.

Zero-Clearance Tablesaw Insert

A

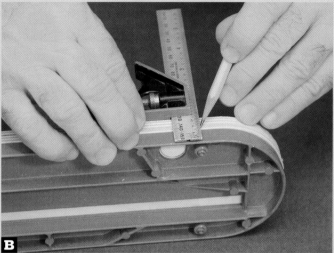

B

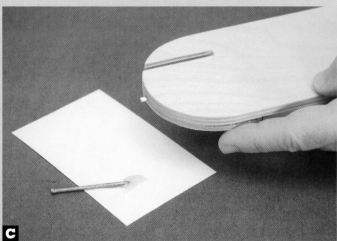

C

D

A ZERO-CLEARANCE TABLESAW INSERT HELPS reduce chipout because it support it supports the wood immediately next to the blade. It's also a safety item because thin strips or cutoffs can't dive past the throatplate.

Although you can buy commercial inserts, they are so easy and inexpensive to craft that you can make one for each blade you own, as well as for each dado width you make.

1. Take your tablesaw's metal insert and attach it with double-faced carpet tape to ½-in. thick plywood. Bandsaw to within ⅛ in. of the perimeter, and finish the edges with a flush-trim bit in your router table, as shown in Photo **A**.

2. Mark the finger hole and the approximate site of the leveling screws, as shown in Photo **B**, and separate the plywood and metal. Drill the finger hole and pilot holes for No. 8 by ⅜-in. flathead screws.

3. Your insert may have a metal pin at the back end to keep it from accidentally lifting. I replicate that detail with a stub of ⅛-in. brass rod glued in a pilot hole, as shown in Photo **C**.

4. Level the insert with your saw table. Set your rip fence over the edge of the insert and raise your running blade through the wood, as shown in Photo **D**. Elevate the blade slightly higher than needed, then lower it to reduce friction and noise.

You can machine a stub mortise and tenon joint with a dado head in your tablesaw or with a table-mounted router.

If you're cutting a rabbet for the panel, use a bit with interchangeable bearings in a variety of diameters. This allows you to widen the rabbet in a series of cuts, minimizing chipout. Start with a large bearing and step toward the smaller diameter that will complete the cut. You can square the rounded corners with a chisel.

You can also make stub tenon doors with the matched pair of router bits shown on p. 153.

Cope-and-Stick Doors

"Cope-and-stick" is the door-construction method usually employed by professional cabinet shops and factories when making raised-panel doors that feature a routed pattern on the inside edges of the rails and stiles. This process involves cutting a recess (a cope) in the end of the stile whose profile matches the routed pattern (the stick) on the inside edge of the rail. That way, the pattern fits in the recess, forming a snug joint with a square corner. Commercial fabricators generally use multihorsepower shapers, but you can get excellent results in your own shop with a table-mounted router and a set of matched bits made specifically for this purpose. There are several molding patterns, so choose the one that best suits the style of your built-in.

A raised-panel door consists of two stiles (the vertical frame members), two rails (the horizontal pieces), plus the panel. To begin this project, you'll want to map out dimensions (see "Sizing the Stiles, Rails, and Panels" below). Then cut and assemble the components.

Sizing the Stiles, Rails, and Panels

THE FIRST THING YOU'LL want to know is what size to cut the blanks. Start with the rails and stiles. Let's assume each door will overlay the face-frame by ½ in. all around the door's perimeter. For example, if the door opening is 11 in. wide by 19 in. high, the overall door size is 12 in. by 20 in. You also need to know the depth of your cope cutter. The Sommerfield Cabinetmaking Set in this demonstration, for example, has a cope depth of ½ in., but your router bits may be different. For easy calculation, we'll choose an apparent stile and rail width of 2 in.—this is the flat surface of the frame, not counting the width (here, ½ in.) of the molded inner edge. So the total width of the rail and stile stock before routing is 2½ in.

The stile length is the overall door height: 20 in. The rail length is the overall door width minus 2 in. for each stile (12 in. − 4 in. = 8 in. in this example).

Calculating the panel dimensions requires a little additional pencil-and-paper work. The raised panel needs space to expand and contract within the frame, so allow ⅛ in. at each edge and end, for a total of ¼ in. less in both width and length. The rail length is 8 in., so subtract ¼ in. to produce a panel width of 7¾ in. The vertical groove-to-groove depth is 16 in., so cut the central panel 15¾ in. long.

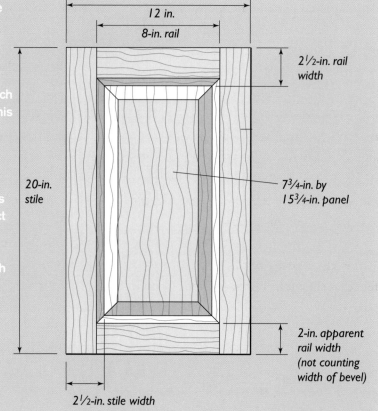

12 in.

8-in. rail

2½-in. rail width

20-in. stile

7¾-in. by 15¾-in. panel

2-in. apparent rail width (not counting width of bevel)

2½-in. stile width

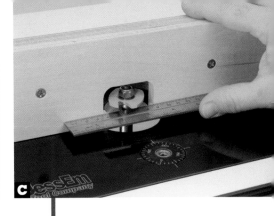

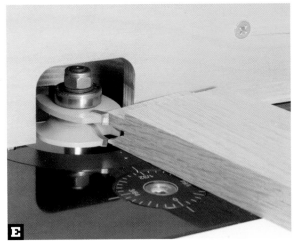

1. Rip and crosscut all the panels to size. Rip and joint the rails and stiles to width and cut the matching parts to identical length. Tape pairs together, as shown in Photo **A**, and slice through both at once with your mitersaw.

2. Put the cope cutter in your router and set its height for a ⅛-in. reveal at the front end of the molding profile. Measure a test piece or use a gauge such as the one from Sommerfeld, as shown in Photo **B**. After you've built a successful door, keep a piece of each test component as a gauge for future setups.

3. Set the bearing of the bit flush with the fence, as shown in Photo **C**, and clamp it securely.

4. Make a follower block from a 8-in.-square piece of ¾-in. plywood. This block helps you push the rail squarely past the cutter and also helps prevent chipout. The center handle shown in the photo isn't absolutely essential, but it does remind you to keep your fingers away from the path of the cutter. Position the good face of the stock against the router table and place the edge against the follower block. For the initial cut, hold the end of the rail about ¼ in. away from the fence, as shown in Photo **D**. This first cut removes most of the waste so your router doesn't have to work as hard when you make the second pass with the rail's end against the fence. Make the cope cuts on the ends of each rail.

5. Switch to the molding (also called sticking or pattern) bit, and align the cutter with the tenon on a coped rail, as shown in Photo **E**. Again, align the bearing with the fence and make a test cut to prove your setup. The ideal joint closes fully without excessive tightness and is flat. Refer to the directions supplied with your bits to solve any problems.

TRADE SECRET

Over the relatively short length of most cabinet doors, the seasonal change in length is negligible, so it's not mandatory to subtract a full ¼ in. when computing the panel length. You do need to be certain, though, that the panel doesn't bottom out in the grooves before the frame joints fully close.

F

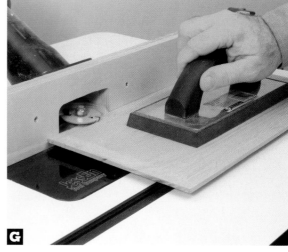

G

6. Dial the speed to its lowest setting (see the sidebar below) and chuck a panel-raising bit in your table-mounted router. Use a fence with a larger opening for this bit. For safety and a smooth cut (and so you don't burn out your router) I suggest you cut the panel in at least three passes. Review the procedures below and fine-tune them based on your router's power, your bit profile, and the density of your wood.

7. Set the cutter's height for your stock thickness. The panel-raising bit I use has two bearings. For the first cuts, you put the large-

diameter bearing between the panel cutter and the back cutter, as shown in Photo **F**.

8. Position the fence flush with the rim of the bearing. After you've made first cuts on all the panels, put the small bearing on the bit and adjust the fence flush with that bit. Make the final cut, as shown in Photo **G**.

If your bit doesn't have replaceable bearings, make a series of cuts, gradually moving the fence closer to the bit. For example, set the fence ⅝ in. from the bearing, make the first cuts on each panel, then move the fence ⅛ in. from the bearing and make the second cut. Finally, set the fence flush with the bearing and finish the panel. Notice how the back cutter trims excess thickness from the rear of the panel so the edges fit into the frame's grooves.

9. Sanding the panel before assembly, as shown in Photo **H**, is a good strategy. So is prestaining. It will ensure seasonal changes don't reveal naked wood along the panel's edges.

10. Assemble the panel and frame without glue to check the fit. Inserting Space Balls® (a brand name of resilient spheres) into the

Watch Your Speed

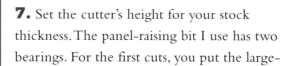

LARGE-DIAMETER BITS CAN DEVELOP dangerously high rim speeds. Some routers have a built-in control that lets you choose a number of speeds. Most, though, require a separate speed control to dial down the speed. Be sure the unit meets or exceeds your tool's amperage draw.

You can't use an external speed control in tandem with a built-in control. Also, the controller may not be compatible with soft-start circuitry (it reduces the motor's initial torque when started). Check with your router's manufacturer to be sure.

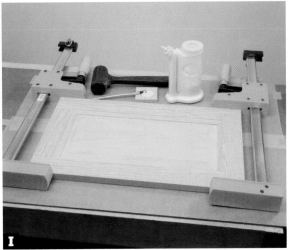

grooves will keep the panel centered and rattle-free. Apply glue to the corner joints, but be careful to avoid excessive amounts so you don't create a clean-up problem or accidentally glue the panel in place. Put the doors together on a flat surface, as shown in Photo **I**, and apply just enough pressure to fully close the joints. Then check the assembly for square

11. If necessary, sand the corner joints so their edges, as well as the front and back faces, are flush. The bit set I used in this demonstration includes a door-edge ogee cutter that complements the curve of the raised panel. Rout the ends, then the edges of each door to produce the result shown in Photo **J**. Note: the profile is wide but quite shallow so it doesn't remove stock needed for Euro hinge cups. If you're making an overlay door, cut the rabbets on the back edges and ends that touch the face frame. Don't rabbet the edges of door pairs that meet without a stile between them.

Glazed doors

The simplest glass door involves a plastic or metal track you purchase before custom-cutting the glass at a local supplier. Visit the glass shop before you start and you'll discover a wide range of choices: clear glass and a whole host of tinted products, patterned and textured glass, varieties that are mirrored, tempered, or laminated, and glass with coatings that block ultraviolet rays to protect the contents of your built-in. Of course, all of those options represent the most basic choices—before you explore the limitless design possibilities offered by stained glass.

Wood-framed glass doors may house a single pane of glass or individual panes (called "lights") separated by a wood framework. An alternative to the challenge of true divided-light construction relies on a wood or synthetic grid set on a

TRADE SECRET

Attempting to cut the molding on the stiles in one pass can stress your router, heat up your bit, and lead to chipout. Fortunately, there's an easy cure. After you've proved the setup with test cuts, move the fence so that the bearing is about 1/8 in. behind the fence. Run all of the stiles through at this setting, then shift the fence flush with the bearing for the final cut.

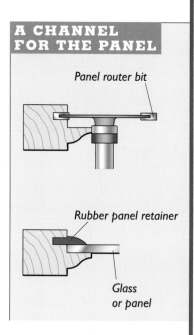

Panel router bit

Rubber panel retainer

Glass or panel

This glass-door router-bit set makes the cope and pattern cuts, as well as a slot for the retainer strip, which is available in clear or dark brown plastic.

single sheet of glass, with the grid mimicking the effect of separate panes. You can attach this grid to the main frame of the door or adhere it to the glass with a few dots of clear silicone.

One set of router bits for glass doors consists of three cutters. The first makes the cope-cut on the ends of the rails, and another, the pattern cutter, shapes the inner perimeter of the frame and cuts the rabbet for the glass at the same time. The third bit cuts a groove for a plastic panel retainer that holds the glass in place. Using the

panel retainer is a great time saver because you otherwise need to cut, shape, finish, and install strips of wood molding to hold the glass in place.

You can also use this three-bit system to install plywood panels. With the panel retainer, you could even change the panels in your doors to give your built-in a makeover with little effort.

Hanging a Door

You have a wide selection of hinges, and you'll find a representative sampling of the various types shown on p. 128. A number of these, such as surface-mount hinges, are easy to install, but it's worth spending some time learning how to mount Euro hinges.

A Euro hinge typically consists of two parts: the hinge cup/arm assembly and the baseplate. You'll usually drill three holes in the door, one for the hinge cup itself and two for the mounting screws. The typical cup hole usually has diameter of 35 mm, and you'll find how deep it should be on the hinge's specification sheet. When you study the specs, you'll note that the offset (the distance from the door's edge) is

Arched-Top Doors

ARCHED-TOP RAISED PANEL DOORS can add an interesting style element to your built-in. To make them, you'll need a set of templates—available in several shapes—that guide the router when forming the panel and upper rail. You need a set of templates because each pair is matched to a specific door width range.

Of course, using the templates involves additional fabrication time, but you may decide that it's a good investment because you'll enjoy the results for a long time.

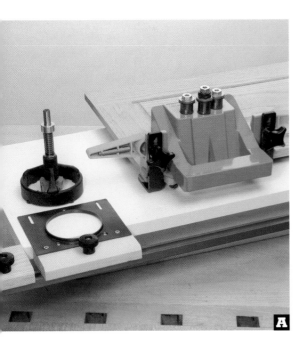

dimensioned to the rim of the cup hole instead of its centerpoint.

Although you can lay out each hole by measuring, a commercial jig will speed your work and improve accuracy at the same time. Virtually any woodworking catalog offers an assortment of hinge-boring jigs. Prices start at about the price tag of a take-out pizza and go up to gourmet dining prices. The key requirements for any jig are that it won't move while you're drilling and that it has a positive depth-stop mechanism. As you pay more for a jig, you'll get more user-friendly features.

The Blum® Ecodrill jig, shown at right in Photo **A**, allows you to literally dial in a variety of offsets using cams set against the door's edge. An additional pair of bits in this jig enables you to drill perfectly-placed 8-mm holes for push-in bushings, which expand by driving a system screw. The other jig in the photo, from Rockler®, costs considerably less but does a fine job of drilling the hinge cup hole.

After you transfer the baseplate centerlines to the carcase, you're ready to drill those mounting holes. Again, a jig is a big convenience, but you must be sure that the hole spacing and backset (distance of the hinge-mounting plate from the front edge of the carcase) matches the hinges you've chosen. The jig from Rockler shown in Photo **B** lets you align the location (marked on tape for easy visibility) with a centerline scribed on the jig's clear baseplate. Drill pilot holes with a self-centering bit and screw the baseplate in position.

Clip the hinge arms onto the baseplates and you're ready to fine-tune the door's fit. Photo **C** shows the driver turning the adjustment screw that sets the door's overlay. The upper screw in the baseplate shifts the door up or down. The rear screw on the hinge arm moves the door in or out.

PRO**TIP**

Always remember that you need to build doors strong enough to survive real-world conditions. In addition, before you start, take an honest reality check of your skill level and the tooling you have. A simple joint made well is better than a complex joint that fits poorly.

DESIGN
OPTIONS

◀ Ribbed glass keeps the "machinery" partially hidden in this appliance garage. The doors tilt forward at the bottom and slide into recesses in the case.

▲ Glass-front doors will do more than make things easier to find. Here, they extend the "windows" in this narrow room, both physically and visually enlarging what otherwise would be wasted space in cramped quarters.

More than any other design element, doors define the style of a room. These quartersawn white oak doors styled with Shaker/Craftsman simplicity, provide a stylistic anchor for the rest of the kitchen.

Proportions matter when building sliding doors. Try to keep their height less than two and a half times their width and make sure your pulls are flush or nearly so.

There's a laundry room behind these frame-and-panel doors, making the best use of a small bath space. When closed, the doors complete the spa-like decorating theme.

DRAWERS

The concept of a drawer seems to be simplicity itself: a five-sided storage box that slides into and out of a larger box. But there are so many different paths from idea to execution it's easy to become overwhelmed by the choices.

To eliminate this anxiety, first decide what you want the drawer to do and choose the drawer-slide hardware. For example, do you need a full-extension slide that provides easy access to contents at the rear, or will a two-thirds extension be adequate? Is a self-closing or anti-slam function important? Then begin asking some aesthetic questions: Are exposed slides acceptable, or do you want to keep the slides hidden to focus attention on the drawer's joinery? As you'll see, drawer slides dictate the drawer's clearances within the carcase and have a strong influence on drawer construction.

After you've made those decisions, you can choose the corner construction method, and that's largely a matter of deciding how much time you're willing to invest in each drawer. ▶ ▶ ▶

The epoxy-coated slide installs easily, works smoothly, and is inexpensive. No wonder it's so popular.

Drawers and Slides

This is a bit difficult for a hardware enthusiast to admit, but there's no absolute rule that you must use drawer-slide hardware. After all, furniture making had a long, glorious history before the invention of metal drawer slides. Even today, some woodworking purists cringe at the idea of attaching anything metallic to one of their creations. If you share that ideology, skip this discussion and go directly to joint-cutting methods. For the vast majority of people, though, using drawer slides makes sense for several compelling reasons:

• You don't need to worry about pulling a drawer out of the carcase, dumping the contents.

• You eliminate wood-to-wood contact, which can be noisy and wear both drawer and carcase.

• You reduce friction, slashing the effort to operate the drawer. That means drawers can carry heavy loads and still slide easily.

• Drawers run straight and true, and unless the slide malfunctions, the drawer won't cock in its opening.

A trio of drawer slides

Manufacturers make drawer slides in a wide range of designs, but three main types will satisfy nearly every requirement for built-ins. These include epoxy-coated slides, side-mounted styles, and bottom-mounted units. As you read about each type, consider the loads your drawers will carry, your budget, and whether concealing the drawer slide is important.

The type of slide you choose will dictate certain critical dimensions of the drawer box. For example, both epoxy-coated and side-mounted slides typically require ½-in. clearance between each side of the drawer box and the carcase. A bottom-mounted slide requires a crucial dimension (usually ½ in.) for the bottom recess between the lower face of the drawer bottom and the mounting surface. The manufacturer's data sheet will usually provide hard measurements for some of the drawer's dimensions, as well as formulas you can use to calculate the remainder. Refer to "Drawer Anatomy" on the facing page to familiarize yourself with the terminology of drawers and slides.

Epoxy-coated slides

The "epoxy-coated" moniker refers to the durable, low-friction coating on the slide components. This style is often called a "Euro slide" because it's engineered to work flawlessly with the standard hole pattern employed in frameless cabinet construction (see "Frameless Cabinets" on p. 49). However, you can easily adapt epoxy-coated slides for face-frame cabinets with simple construction techniques (see "Install epoxy-coated slides" on p. 99).

Epoxy-coated slides make a great choice for kitchen drawers, and these slides are easy to find at home centers or even a well-stocked hardware store. Many mail-order suppliers provide a more comprehensive selection of lengths, however, and colors other than white. For heavy-duty work, look for a quality upgrade that nearly doubles the typical 55-lb. load rating to 100 lb.

The photo, at right, provides an example of a single-extension slide: It allows only a part of the drawer's total length to extend past the front of the carcase. Extension ratios of ⅔ and ¾ are common. A 12-in. slide with a ¾ extension ratio, for example, will move the drawer forward 9 in. The remaining 3 in. is called the extension loss.

Epoxy-coated slides open and close smoothly, and many include a "self-closing" feature. When the drawer is within about 2 in. of being shut, it rolls down a slope in the slide to help pull the box closed. In addition, the L-shaped drawer member of this type of slide wraps around the side and bottom of the drawer, which not only provides secure support, but also allows most, though not all, of the drawer side to be seen.

Side-mounted slides

There are several types of slides made for installation on the sides of drawers, but for our discussion, we'll define a side-mounted slide as a heavy-duty unit with a ball-bearing action. The load rating of side-mounted slides usually begins at 75 lb. to 100 lb. and goes upward from there. For extreme loads, you can even install more than one set of slides on the drawer side.

You'll find these slides in single-extension, full-extension, and over-extension versions.

Full-extension slides maximize your access to the drawer's entire contents, an absolute necessity in many applications. For example, if you fill a drawer with CDs, you'll want a full-extension slide because being able to see only two-thirds of your music collection isn't very helpful.

Over-extension slides provide a remedy where an obstruction, such an overhanging countertop, restricts easy access to the back of the

Smooth operation, impressive weight ratings, and the availability of full-extension are three good reasons to choose side-mounted slides.

DRAWER ANATOMY

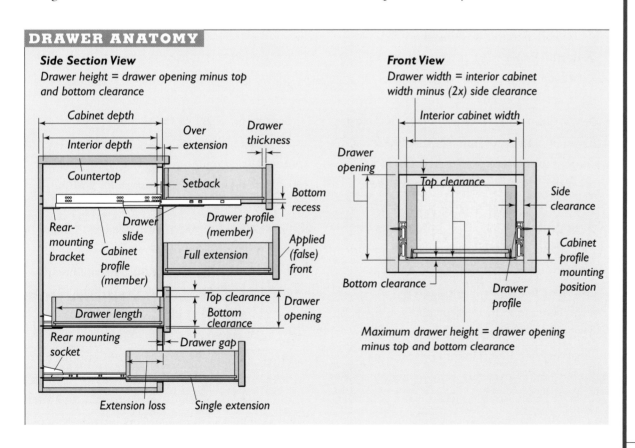

Side Section View
Drawer height = drawer opening minus top and bottom clearance

Cabinet depth
Interior depth
Over extension
Drawer thickness
Countertop
Setback
Bottom recess
Drawer slide
Rear-mounting bracket
Cabinet profile (member)
Drawer profile (member)
Applied (false) front
Full extension
Top clearance
Drawer opening
Bottom clearance
Drawer length
Rear mounting socket
Drawer gap
Extension loss
Single extension

Front View
Drawer width = interior cabinet width minus (2x) side clearance

Interior cabinet width
Drawer opening
Top clearance
Side clearance
Cabinet profile mounting position
Bottom clearance
Drawer profile

Maximum drawer height = drawer opening minus top and bottom clearance

As a rule of thumb, drawer boxes are about 3 in. shorter than the overall cabinet depth. For example, that means 21-in. drawers for a base cabinet that's 24 in. deep. This sizing usually provides adequate clearance for rear-mounted drawer support sockets in face-frame cabinets, but you should always consult the slide manufacturer's specifications before you start cutting lumber.

If you're absolutely determined to wring every cubic inch of storage space out of your cabinet, you may be able to make longer drawers, but consider making a mockup to verify clearances and extension.

drawer. They often feature a progressive action: Sections extend in succession to the full reach.

Side-mounted slides aren't a good choice when you want to show off fancy corner joinery because they can block a significant portion of the drawer's sides. Many, however, come with a self-closing feature, as well as a detent that keeps the drawer firmly closed. Ball bearings make the action smooth and quiet and account for the excellent load-carrying capacity of these slides. They may not be widely stocked in "big box" stores, so you may need to find a mail-order source. Be prepared, however—a full-extension side-mounted slide will carry a price tag typically twice that of its epoxy-coated counterpart.

Bottom-mounted slides

For right now, we're going to focus our attention on a specific bottom-mount slide, the Tandem slide made by Blum, in both its single- and full-extension versions. Whichever you choose, this slide hides discreetly under the drawer so it's invisible under most circumstances. It's a great choice for showing off fancy joinery.

The top-of-the-line Tandem is not only a full-extension model, but also includes a closing refinement named Blumotion®—a gas-filled cylinder built into the slide to ensure soft self-closing. To shut a drawer, you simply give it a shove (from tender to angry), and the system activates as the drawer travels into the carcase.

The cylinder's braking action reacts proportionally to the force you apply, so the drawer slows down, then gently and silently stops. It's really a fascinating movement, and you'll be tempted to try different closing speeds to try to fool the slide into slamming. (You can't.) Watching the drawer shut is like viewing a silent movie. You can also install Blumotion cylinders to close doors noiselessly (see p. 130).

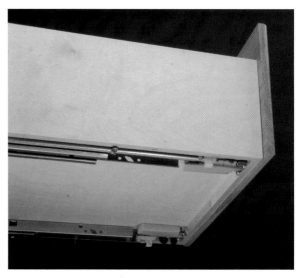

Whether you want to show off fancy joinery or simply want an uncluttered look, bottom-mounted slides help achieve your goal.

This Tandem slide incorporates two adjustments that fine-tune the fit of the drawer. One moves the drawer face upward a maximum of ⅛ in., and the other permits you to tilt the top of the drawer front forward. These adjustments facilitate the positioning of overlay drawer fronts, of course, but really shine when you're installing inlay drawers, which look best when flush to the carcase with even reveals on all sides.

Not surprisingly, all the technological refinements of the Blumotion slide translate into a premium price: several times that of a side-mounted full-extension slide. The Blum slides without Blumotion are less expensive, and the price of a single-extension model called Solo competes with side-mounted full-extension slides.

For the sake of completeness, I've included two additional kinds of bottom-mounted slides, pictured on p. 130 in the "Hardware" chapter. Both of them are good designs and will give you serviceable results.

Drawer-Box Construction

Once you have your slides in hand, you'll be ready to finalize the size of each box by using the carcase dimensions and manufacturer's data sheet to achieve the proper clearances. But before you start building drawers, you'll need to make some decisions about joinery and materials.

You can also consider skipping the construction step entirely by subcontracting the construction of the drawers (see "Custom Drawers by Mail Order or Computer" below).

Joinery

When deciding what joinery you'll use for the corners of the drawers, it's a good time to remind yourself that the significance of the drawer lies primarily in its ability to hold items, not in its function as a design element. Even though some woodworkers understand that, they sometimes get carried away with intricate joinery that requires painstaking craftsmanship visible only briefly as the drawer flashes open and shut.

If you're willing to invest the time to build your skills making fancy drawers, have at it and enjoy the process. But don't hold back on making built-ins because you can't cut fancy joints. You can make perfectly serviceable drawers with the regular blade in your tablesaw or with a table-mounted router bit at only one setting.

Choosing between drawer sides of solid lumber or plywood involves both aesthetic and practical considerations.

Custom Drawers by Mail Order or Computer

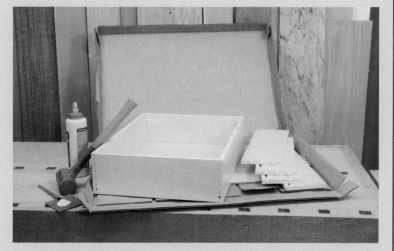

THERE ARE A NUMBER of companies that produce drawers in stock sizes or will custom-build them to your specifications. The components usually arrive knocked down and ready for assembly. Doweled joints are common, but you can order dovetailed drawers. Metal drawer sides with built-in glides are specially engineered for frameless cabinets.

Farm out some of the work for your built-in by ordering ready-to-assemble custom drawers.

Solid-Front Drawer

This vintage drawer features a one-piece front joined to the sides with half-blind dovetails.

When we get into the joinery later in the chapter, we'll cover simple joints first, dovetails later.

Drawer materials

You'll fashion most drawer boxes from ½-in.-thick stock, but one of the first decisions you'll need to make is whether that means solid lumber or plywood. Box joints, dovetails, and other fancy joinery methods virtually demand solid-wood construction. You could theoretically make dovetails in plywood, of course, but the juxtaposition of a traditional joint with modern materials would be visually disconcerting.

Solid wood

Solid lumber is the traditional choice for drawer boxes, and you'll definitely want to choose it if you'll cut fancy joints. Even in high-end cabinetry, though, builders typically choose an inexpensive secondary wood for the drawer box and other concealed parts and reserve the fancy lumber for visible elements.

Many cabinetmakers choose poplar for the drawer box because it's an inexpensive hardwood that's reasonably stable and machines cleanly. Depending upon market conditions in your region, your supplier may be able to get another species with similar properties at a lower cost.

Pine and other softwoods retailed as "drawer stock" can often be pricey, and the lumber usually doesn't cut as cleanly as hardwood or offer its dent resistance. The high pitch content in softwoods can sometimes produce a blotchy-looking finish, especially under stains, and in severe cases, the wood can bleed enough sap to make the contents of the drawer sticky.

With both hardwoods and softwoods, you'll have all of the challenges associated with solid lumber, such as knots, twisting, warping, cupping, and other defects. Finding wide stock that's flat can often be a problem, and gluing up narrow boards into the widths you need requires several time-consuming machining operations.

Plywood

Plywood's cross-banded veneer construction helps stabilize it in seasonal changes in humidity. Plywood also eliminates the preparation solid wood requires, including jointing and surface and thickness planing. Simply rip and crosscut your pieces, and you're ready for corner joinery.

The problem with hardwood and softwood plywoods is their usual prevalence of voids and lack of uniformity in the thickness of their plies, which makes their edge appearance unappealing.

Baltic birch plywood provides a solution, and 12-mm sheets are a close metric equivalent of ½-in. solid lumber. Because its nine plies rarely have voids, and because the material machines well and finishes nicely, it's no surprise that Baltic birch is a popular choice for internal drawer components. The grain pattern (figure) of the wood is quite bland, but that's appropriate for a part that's rarely seen. For more information about Baltic birch plywood, see p. 25.

Building Drawer Boxes

Making drawers is a process that can take advantage of production-line techniques to save you time and energy. To receive the maximum benefits, though, you'll need to invest some time up-front, making a detailed cut list and planning your machining setups.

Making drawers from solid stock can require a considerable amount of time for stock preparation. Here's the basic sequence of operations:

• Surface-plane one face of each board flat with your jointer.

- Run each board through your planer to make the second face flat and parallel to the first.

- Joint one edge of each board so it's straight and square.

- If the stock is wide enough to produce your drawer parts, you can rip it to width with your tablesaw and smooth that cut with your jointer.

- If you need to edge-join lumber, rip a straight edge, joint, then glue and clamp.

- After the glue dries, scrape and sand the joints, and check that the board is flat. If it's not, you'll need to plane one face flat, then plane the opposite face parallel.

- Rip edge-joined pieces to the required widths and joint the cut edges.

- If you have a thickness sander, you can run both sides of all the stock through it to bring the wood to an absolutely consistent thickness and to remove all planer marks.

Proportioning Drawers

SIZING A BANK OF DRAWERS MEANS MORE THAN figuring the maximum available height and dividing it by the number of drawers you want. The resulting uniformity will mimic the appearance of a stack of bricks—it's functionally acceptable, but it doesn't look quite right. That's because our eyes and brain work together, and their combined visual experience tells us that a stack is more stable when the objects graduate in size: large on bottom, small on top. Here's an easy procedure that will help you design a set of drawers with pleasing proportions. Bear in mind that what we're really doing here is sizing the drawer openings—you'll need to then take into account your hardware and other fitting considerations before you build the actual drawer boxes.

This procedure is easy to remember, and it works with either an even or odd number of drawers. For the sake of easy arithmetic, we'll say that each drawer opening in the stack is 1 in. taller than the one above it. Of course, you can make the increment any amount you want, but 1 in. usually seems to work well.

Referring to the drawing, you'll see that the overall opening is 27 in. from the bottom of the top rail to the top of the bottom rail, but you also need to subtract the total dimensions of the intermediate rails (three in this four-drawer stack), here ¾ in. each, for a total of 2¼ in.. This leaves the total height of the four drawer openings at 24¾ in. (27−2¼ = 24¾ in.).

Now, calculate the drawer sizes: the top drawer is x, the second is x + 1 in., and so on. Add up the sizes, and the total is 4x + 6 in. = 24¾ in. Subtracting 6 in. from both sides of the equation gives you 4x = 24 ¾ in.. Dividing both sides by 4 then tells

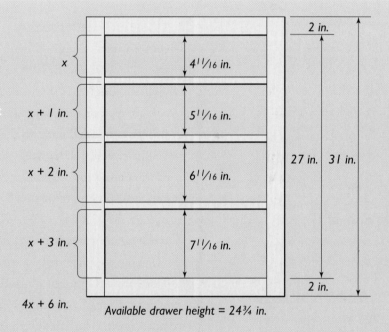

x

$x + 1$ in.

$x + 2$ in.

$x + 3$ in.

$4x + 6$ in.

$4^{11}/_{16}$ in.

$5^{11}/_{16}$ in.

$6^{11}/_{16}$ in.

$7^{11}/_{16}$ in.

2 in.

27 in. | 31 in.

2 in.

Available drawer height = 24¾ in.

you that $x = 4^{11}/_{16}$, which is the size of the top drawer opening. Adding 1 in. to each of the next drawers gives the results shown in the drawing.

In most applications the math works out very neatly. But sometimes you'll discover that division and rounding can make the calculated total slightly more or less than the actual measurement. For example, you may find that the calculated total in a five-drawer stack is ¹⁄₁₆ in. short of the measurement. Rather than adding 0.0125 in. to each drawer opening, simply add the entire ¹⁄₁₆ in. to one of the openings. No one will ever be able to tell.

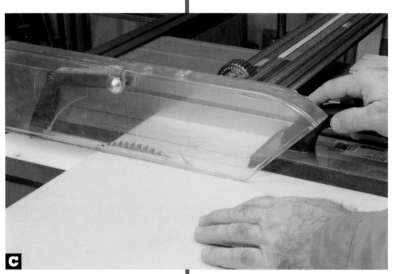

Choosing Baltic birch plywood, however, lets you skip virtually all the steps above. For the following demonstrations I'll use 12-mm Baltic birch plywood (approximately ½ in. thick).

Cutting drawer blanks

1. The factory edges of plywood panels are usually straight enough to guide rip cuts, but not clean enough for a finished surface. To remind myself to cut away these edges later, I use a lumber crayon to mark the face of the panel along both factory edges, parallel to the grain, as shown in Photo **A**.

2. I'll usually make the first cut with a circular saw to rip the panel approximately in half, which reduces its weight and bulk. Of course, you'll want to make sure that the resulting pieces are wide enough to produce the drawer widths you need. As you can see in Photo **B**,

a straightedge guide keeps the cut on track. Depending on the accuracy of your setup, you may be satisfied with this cut quality as a finished edge. If not, mark the edges with the lumber crayon.

3. Rip all the sides (front and back, too) to the proper width, as shown in Photo **C**. The back will end up narrower, but you'll cut it to final size later to create a drawer with a removable bottom. (See the "Trade Secret" on p. 95.)

4. Crosscut a pair of sides and a pair of ends for each drawer, as shown in Photo **D**. Use a stopblock setup or gang-cut taped stacks to ensure identical lengths. If you're working with solid wood, mark the outside of each piece with masking tape, as shown in "Choosing Sides" on p. 99. With plywood components,

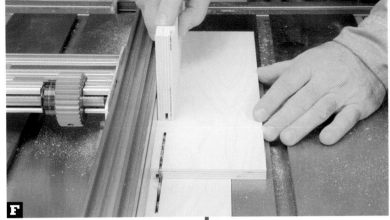

choosing one side instead of the other is mostly a matter of appearance.

5. The usual stock for drawer bottoms is nominal ¼-in. plywood. The Baltic-birch "equivalent" is composed of 5 plies and measures 6 mm thick. Rather than going to the trouble of creating a setup that cuts this groove for the bottom board in one pass, you'll probably find that it's more efficient to groove the drawer-box members with two passes of your standard tablesaw blade. Begin the setup shown in Photo **E** by setting your blade ¼ in. high, and lock the fence ¼ in. from the inner side of the blade. (If you've chosen bottom-mounted slides, refer to the hardware data sheet to set the correct bottom recess.) Set the back aside for now, and cut a groove in the inner face of all the fronts and sides.

6. Slide the fence away from the blade so the second pass will make a cut wide enough to accommodate the plywood bottom in a smooth sliding fit, as shown in Photo **F**. With most tablesaw fences, you'll set the fence position by trial and error, using the "knock and lock" method. With the Incra® fence on my saw, I had to do that only once. Now, every time I make drawers, I refer to the setting I recorded and lock it down immediately. Whatever fence you're using, make this cut in the front and two sides of each drawer.

7. Without changing the location of the fence, elevate the blade to cut completely through the stock. Rip the back of the drawer to its finished width, as shown in Photo **G**.

TRADE SECRET

A drawer bottom fit into a groove on all sides makes sense from a production standpoint—the back and front are identical. But I prefer a removable bottom. First, you can take it out to simplify finishing the drawer, and second, you can easily replace it if it gets damaged. These advantages make the removable bottom my first choice whenever possible.

PROTIP

Choosing a water-resistant glue for drawer assembly will help ensure that joints stay tight, even in high-humidity areas such as kitchens and baths.

Drawer Joinery

At this point, you could assemble a drawer with butt joints, glued and stapled. Using butt-joint construction, you can cut and assemble enough drawers for a good-size built-in while the elitist is still tinkering with the setup of his complicated jig. However, there are alternatives almost as easy.

Drawer-lock joint

A drawer-lock joint increases the glue surface of a joint and provides you a mechanical registration so it assembles quickly, positively, and with less tendency for sliding under gluing pressure.

Despite the joint's name, it is not a true interlocking device, so you still need glue, fasteners, or both to keep the assembly secure. However, the joint's design does provide some structural reinforcement so its strength is not solely dependant on glue and fasteners.

To cut this joint, you need to hold some pieces on end on the router table as you guide them through the cutter. A tall fence will give you maximum control (see "Make a Tall Router Table Fence" on the facing page).

1. Cut your drawer sides and ends to size, and slice the groove for the bottom in each piece. Chuck the drawer-lock bit into your table-mounted router—it cannot be used in a hand-held tool. Adjust the bit's height and projection from the fence, as shown in Photo **A**, to match the set-up block that's usually available from the bit's manufacturer. If the set-up block isn't matched to your stock's thickness, you may need to perform some trial-and-error adjustment of the fence position. Even with a set-up block, it's a good idea to cut a few test joints in scrap stock to verify the settings.

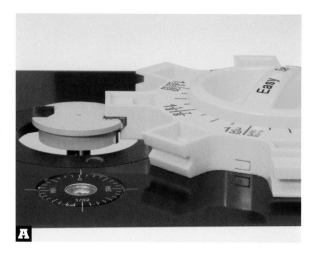

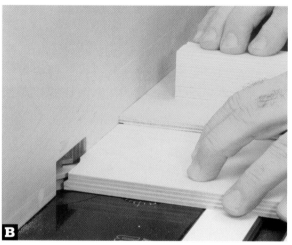

2. Lay a drawer front on your router table with the groove for the bottom against the table. Turn on the router, and push the end of the stock past the cutter. A simple push block similar to that shown in Photo **B** will help prevent tearout where the bit exits the wood. When you've proved the setup, repeat the cut at the other end and at both ends of the back.

3. Without changing the setup, position the grooved inner face of a drawer side against the tall fence and rout the inside end, as shown in Photo **C**. The vertical push block makes it easy to keep the piece upright and to apply even pressure against the fence.

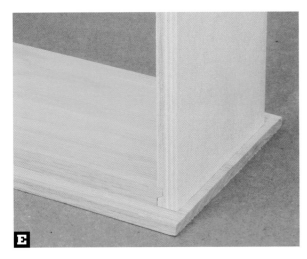

4. Test-fit the pieces, as shown in Photo **D**. If the end of the front overhangs the side, move the fence so it covers more of the bit. If the joint is too tight, lower the bit. Continue to make test cuts until you're satisfied with the fit, then cut the joints in all your drawer pieces.

5. To make a drawer front with a lip similar to the one shown in Photo **E**, rout the sides first, and then move the fence away from the bit in ⅛-in. increments, gradually deepening the cut to the depth you want. Use a dado head or straight router bit to shape the square-edged lip at the top and bottom of the front.

Make a Tall Router-Table Fence

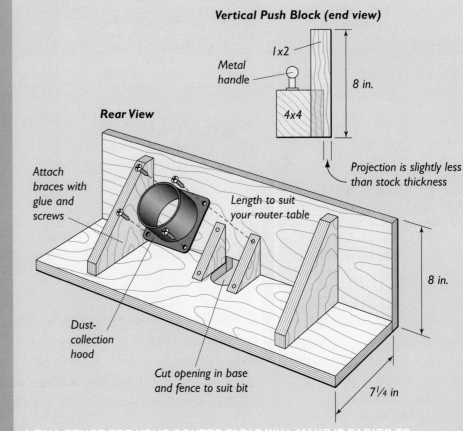

Vertical Push Block (end view)

1x2
Metal handle
8 in.
4x4

Projection is slightly less than stock thickness

Rear View

Attach braces with glue and screws

Length to suit your router table

Dust-collection hood

Cut opening in base and fence to suit bit

8 in.

7¼ in

A TALL FENCE FOR YOUR ROUTER TABLE WILL MAKE IT EASIER TO machine the ends of pieces. Baltic birch plywood that's ¾-in. thick is a great material for this fence, and assembling it with glue and screws will keep it sturdy for years. Make the opening for the bit as small as possible while still allowing the cutter to spin freely. An overly large opening can snag pieces as you're guiding them and also reduces the efficiency of your dust-collection system.

TRADE SECRET

Don't get carried away when sanding the outer drawer sides after assembly. A typical clearance is ½-in. per side, and most slides have a finicky tolerance range. Your drawer may look slick but not have a movement to match if you sand past the point of your slide's tolerance range.

Assembling the drawer

1. Glue and clamp the drawer upside down on a flat surface, and carefully check it for square, as shown in Photo **F**.

2. Measure the plywood bottom, cut it to size, and slide it into place. Don't apply glue to the bottom or the grooves. Drill pilot holes, and fasten the bottom to the back with No. 8 by ¾-in. roundhead screws, as shown in Photo **G**.

3. To speed production, shoot brads or narrow-crown staples through the sides into the front and back, as shown in Photo **H**, and then you can unclamp the drawer. Driving pairs of fasteners at opposing angles improves their holding power. Set the drawer on a flat surface to

ensure you don't introduce any rack (twist) into the assembly.

4. After the drawers dry, soften the edges to make them more user-friendly. Chuck a ⅛-in. roundover bit into your table router, as shown in Photo **I**. Rout the full inner perimeter of the box, but skip the outside front edges and ends. This will preserve square corners to mate with the false front.

Installing Drawer Slides

All of the careful work you've put into your built-in really pays off when it comes time to install the drawer slides. That's because trouble-free installation depends upon a carcase and drawers that are square, made to tolerance, and free of racking. If you meet all of those conditions, drawer installation will be fast and routine.

If you do run into problems, keep cool and think your way out of the situation. A binding drawer could mean the mounting surfaces in your carcase may not be parallel, either vertically or horizontally. Or it could point to a drawer that's out of square.

Install epoxy-coated slides

1. In the slide package, you'll find four major pieces for each drawer. Some manufacturers, like Blum, clearly mark each to eliminate confusion, as shown in Photo **A**. The one marked DR mounts on the right side of the drawer, and CR identifies the member that you fasten to the right side of the cabinet.

2. Invert a drawer, and position the drawer members flush with the front of the box. Drill pilot holes to reduce the risk of splitting—a self-centering drill bit is ideal for this job. Photo **B** shows how you drive screws into the drawer's side, bottom, or both.

3. Blum is one manufacturer that produces a jig to make slide-mounting easier. The jig isn't mandatory, but it eliminates tedious and repetitive marking. For the Model 230 slides in this demonstration, snap the cabinet member into the gun-shaped jig, as shown in Photo **C**. That position automatically produces a 2-mm set-back from the front plane of the carcase.

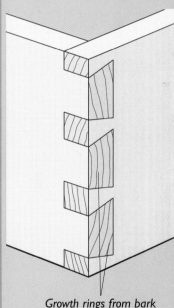

Growth rings from bark side of tree face toward interior of box.

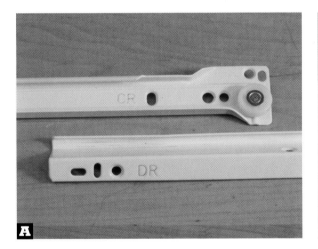

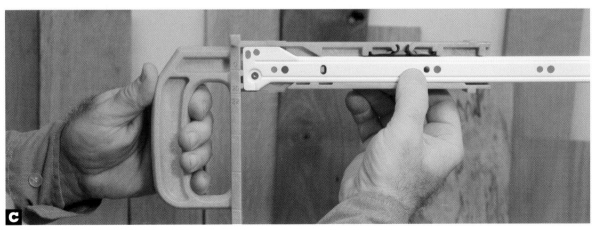

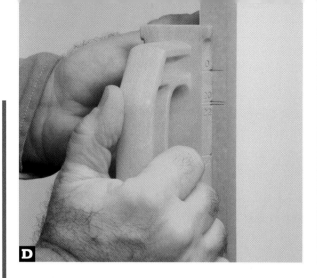

D

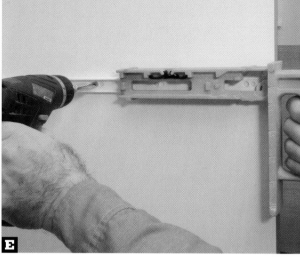

E

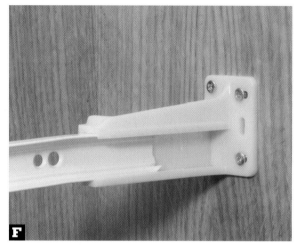

F

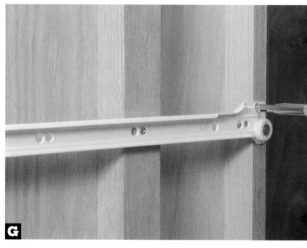

G

TRADE SECRET

Just as ice cream is available in more flavors than vanilla, you'll find drawer slides in colors other than white and chrome. Check several online and mail-order sources instead of merely settling for the first item you find.

4. Run a strip of masking tape down the front edge of the carcase, and mark the position of the drawers. When you align the jig, as shown in Photo **D**, the bottom of the drawer will be at the 20-mm mark and the top of the false front for the next drawer will be at the 22-mm line.

5. Drill pilot holes into the carcase, and drive the mounting screws, as indicated in Photo **E**. Twisting the jig separates it from the hardware, and you're ready to install the other cabinet member by snapping it into the opposite side of the jig. Test-fit the drawer.

6. If you're working with a face-frame cabinet, you'll use the installation jig to position and install the front end of the cabinet member. One way of installing the back end of the

slide involves a press-on plastic socket from the slide's manufacturer, such as the one shown in Photo **F**. If you go this route, install blocking behind the cabinet's back (if you have clearance for it) or inside the carcase to provide a solid anchoring point for the screws.

7. In some other situations, you may be able to install blocks on the sides of the carcase to which you can attach the cabinet members. Use shop-made blocks, as shown in Photo **G**, or a manufactured adjustable plastic version.

Install side-mounted slides

You'll typically use centerlines to install side-mounted slides. For the full-extension Accuride® slide in this demonstration, install the drawer members on a centerline 1¼ in. from the bottom edge of the drawer, while the cabinet member is

Dovetailed Drawers

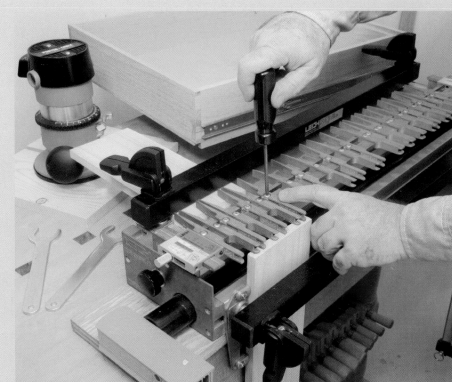

DOVETAILS WILL HOLD DRAWERS TOGETHER efficiently even if the glue fails completely—a common event before modern adhesives. Although high-tech glues have eliminated a practical reason for dovetails, their appearance continues to fascinate, and they have become a touchstone of quality.

To help you cut a number of dovetailed drawers, consider investing in a jig you can use with a router. Every woodworking catalog offers several types. The simplest produce half-blind dovetails at a fixed spacing. More expensive models allow you to vary the spacing between the pins and also to handle wider stock. The high-end jigs also add the capacity for cutting through-dovetails.

Buying a dovetail jig does not guarantee success. You have to be willing to devote the time to learn how your jig works, to cut sample joints to perfect your technique, and to zero in on the precise adjustments of both the jig and router. If you're willing to invest the money and time, however, you can turn out crisp joints that will never fail to produce admiring comments

centered on a line 1½ in. from the bottom of the drawer. The difference between these two positions creates a ¼-in. bottom clearance.

1. Separate the slide members from each other by moving the disconnect lever, shown in Photo **A**, and pulling.

2. Draw the centerline for the cabinet member, as shown in Photo **B**. You can use a framing square for this job, but I've found that a drafting square is faster because it's easy to register against the front of the cabinet.

3. Drill pilot holes, and drive screws through the horizontal slots to install the cabinet member. As you can see in Photo **C** on p. 102, the front end of the cabinet member is flush with the front plane of the carcase.

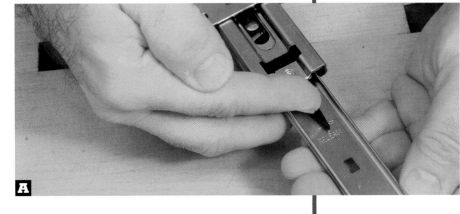

A

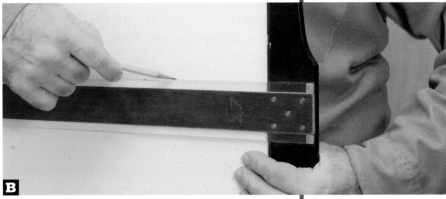

B

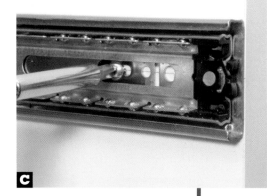

C

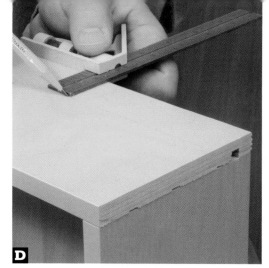

D

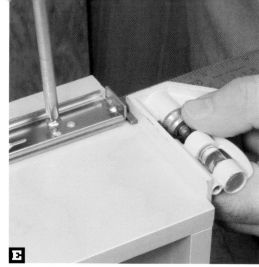

E

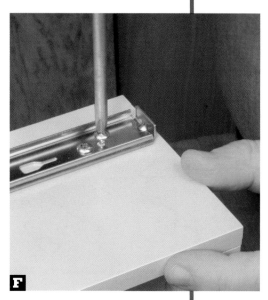

F

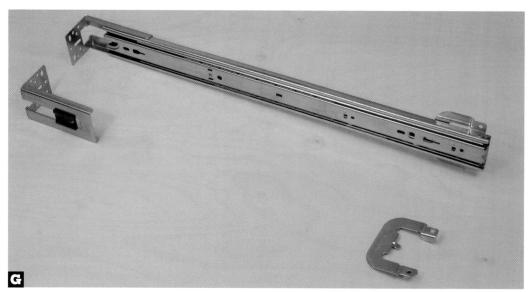

G

4. Use a combination square to draw the drawer member centerline, as shown in Photo **D**.

5. Referring to Photo **E**, set a small combination square to gauge the setback of the drawer member from the front of the box. For an overlay drawer, this setback is ⅛ in. Drill pilot holes, and drive screws through the vertical slots to secure these parts.

6. Slide the drawer members into the cabinet members to check the fit and action. To move the drawer vertically, reposition the screws in the drawer-member slots. The slots in the cabinet members permit front-to-back adjustment. When you're satisfied with the alignment, lock

the settings by driving screws into the round holes, as shown in Photo **F**.

7. When you use this type of slide with a face-frame cabinet, purchase a kit of side and rear brackets for each pair of slides. This additional hardware, shown in Photo **G**, helps ensure secure connections. Be sure to add blocking at the back to furnish a solid target for the rear bracket screws.

Install bottom-mounted slides

1. Carefully follow the manufacturer's specifications when you build the drawer boxes. Drill a 6-mm hole in the back of the drawer to accept the hook on the back of each drawer runner. You could lay out each hole position by measurement, but Blum's Tandem drilling template eliminates that work, and the stop collar on the bit ensures consistent results, as shown in Photo **H**.

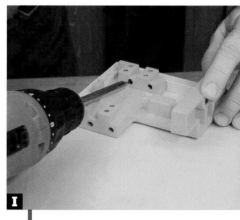

2. Set the stop collar on the 2.5-mm bit so it projects 10-mm (about ⅜ in.) out of the template. Referring to Photo **I**, firmly hold the template in the front corner of the drawer, and drill the two angled pilot holes. Repeat at the other front corner.

3. Mount the left and right locking devices by driving the screws into the pilot holes. The locking devices, shown in Photo **J**, are the standard model for use with overlay drawer fronts. There are special devices for inset drawers and narrow drawers, and another for applications like roll-out trays where a precise stopping position is required.

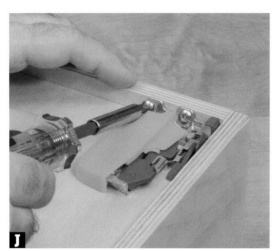

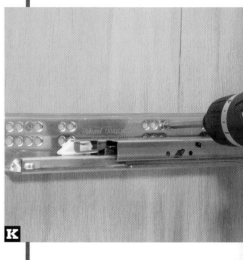

4. Use a drafting square to mark the mounting position of the runners, and install them to the side of the carcase, as shown in Photo **K**.

5. To install the drawer, simply place the box on the runners and close it. The locking devices connect automatically to the runners. To remove the drawer, squeeze the orange handles on the locking devices and pull the drawer out and up. The finished installation in Photo **L** shows how the hardware is invisible from normal viewing perspectives.

6. For face-frame cabinets, attach a bracket to the back of the cabinet to support the runner profiles. Photo **M** shows blocking installed inside the cabinet, making a solid target for mounting screws.

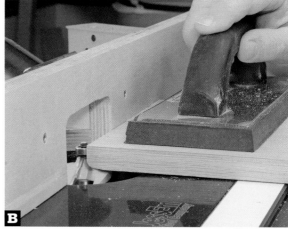

WHAT CAN GO WRONG

The length of a drawer front must often match the width of a door. Making doors is usually the more difficult of the two operations, so it's best to tackle that task first. That way, making a drawer front that's a perfect size match involves only a simple crosscut instead of resizing the multiple pieces of a door.

Making Drawer Fronts

Now that you've made and installed the drawer box, it's time to make the part that will be seen: the drawer front. From a design perspective, it's essential that the drawer harmonizes with the doors on your built-in. This means that both the doors and drawers are made from the same material and have the same thickness. Edge profiles do not need to be absolutely identical, but they must complement each other. If your built-in has raised-panel doors, for example, the drawer edge profile will usually echo the sweep of the panel edges.

The drawer fronts will also take their size cues from the doors, sharing the same amount of overlay, if any. In addition, if a drawer is above a door (as in a base cabinet, for example), the length of a drawer front will be identical to the width of the door.

In the following demonstration, you'll see how to make a drawer front from solid stock so it harmonizes with a raised-panel door.

1. Rip and crosscut the drawer-front blanks to size. Choose the router bit for the edge profile. In this case, the drawer-edge profile shown in

Photo **A** is part of a set of bits, so there's no worry about stylistic compatibility between the doors and drawers. Chuck the bit into your table-mounted router, and use a straightedge to ensure the edge of the bit is aligned with the face of your fence.

2. Set the bit height so the first cut removes a modest amount of stock. As Photo **B** illustrates, make the first cuts on the ends of the stock, then rout the long edges.

3. Raise the bit in increments no greater than ⅛ in., and continue the routing procedure until you've shaped the full profile, as shown in Photo **C**.

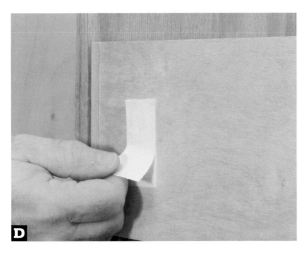

D

E

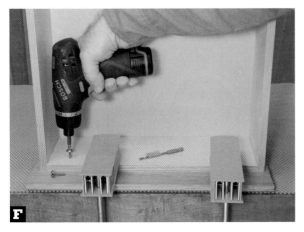

F

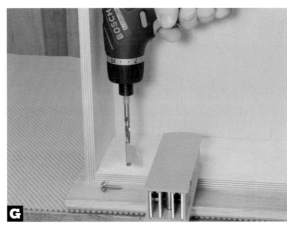

G

Install the drawer fronts

1. You'll attach the false front to a drawer after the box is installed in the cabinet. Place a couple of pieces of double-faced cloth carpet tape on the drawer front, as shown in Photo **D**, and pull the box slightly back from the front plane of the cabinet.

2. This next step is easier with a helper, but you can also do it solo. Position the drawer front on the cabinet and slide the drawer firmly forward to adhere it to the front, as shown in Photo **E**. If the drawer front is inset, use spacers around its perimeter to set the reveal. Carefully remove the drawer.

3. As Photo **F** illustrates, clamp the drawer and front to your workbench, being careful not to shift the parts. Drill pilot holes and drive screws with large heads to unite the assembly. Truss-head screws are ideal, but roundhead or panhead screws will be fine.

4. Replace the drawer to inspect the fit. If you need to tweak the alignment of the false front, remove it from the drawer box and strip away the tape. Enlarge the holes through the drawer front with a ¼-in. bit, as shown in Photo **G**, and start two screws in their original holes in the false front. You'll now probably have enough adjustment room to align the front. Drive the remaining screws after the alignment is perfect.

PRO TIP

When working with solid-wood stock, always rout the chip-prone end grain first. Routing the long edges will usually remove any tear-out from those first cuts.

PRO TIP

As an alternative to adding blocking inside the cabinet, you could add blocking behind the rear panel if you'll have enough clearance after installation.

DESIGN
OPTIONS

▸ Modifying a traditional style can increase the practicality of a drawer design. Here, a Shaker style is mimicked in the graduated configuration of the drawers, but the top faces are really one, built to accommodate larger items.

▲ When convention won't do the trick, try thinking "inside the box." A cubby makes a personalized storage space for newspapers and magazines for the avid reader.

With a little forethought, you'll find space for drawers in the most imaginative and useful places. These deep drawers under the bench seats are great hiding places for bulky items that see infrequent use.

Careful planning and a thorough analysis of storage needs were a necessary requisite to creating this useful and cozy bedroom "suite."

When a pull-out drawer won't do, try tilting the design to fit large packages.

COUNTERTOPS

A countertop usually has a major impact on the appearance of your built-in: Its scale alone makes it a big attention grabber. In addition to functioning as an important design element, the countertop provides a useful space for activities and serves as a backdrop for decorative accessories you place on it.

Distributors carry an amazing range of countertop materials from which you can choose: solid wood, plywood, laminate, synthetic solid surfaces, concrete, ceramic tile, stone tile, polished stone slabs, and more. And within each of those categories you can select from a broad spectrum of designs, colors, textures, and finishes.

This chapter will introduce you to the scope of choices, as well as provide information that will help you narrow the field to those materials best suited to your project. In addition, you'll see a hands-on demonstration of the steps involved in making and installing a laminate countertop. ▶ ▶ ▶

Selecting a Countertop

Choosing the right countertop material means balancing a number of factors, including aesthetics, functionality, and budget. In addition, the workability of the material will also figure in your decision. Some materials will allow you to fabricate and install them yourself. Other products, though, will limit your exertion to handing over your credit card.

Plywood and solid wood

Hardwood plywood—with a banded edge to hide the layered core—is one of the most economical choices. It makes a good countertop for a low-usage installation, but can quickly show dents and scratches if subjected to heavy wear. Even though it's called hardwood ply, that name comes from its thin and fragile decorative face veneer. The inner plies are generally made from a softwood species, which doesn't provide much backup resistance to dings and dents.

A solid wood countertop, on the other hand, especially one made from a hardwood species, can overcome many of plywood's shortcomings.

At the same time, though, solid wood introduces a number of other issues. While plywood is quite dimensionally stable, solid wood moves in response to seasonal changes in humidity. You must accommodate this inevitable movement or risk cracking the countertop. Fabrication can also be quite challenging—you must carefully surface the lumber, arrange the boards for a good match of color and figure, and joint the edges to achieve nearly invisible glue joints. Finishing solid wood can also be demanding because a large flat surface can highlight any imperfections.

Laminates

High-pressure plastic laminates reigned as the nearly universal countertop material for decades. And despite the growing popularity of other materials, laminates still command an enormous marketshare. According to industry estimates, laminates account for 80 percent or more of countertop purchases. Its popularity comes as no surprise—it's available in a huge array of colors, patterns, and textures; it's durable and wears well under normal use (though it will scratch and show burn marks); it's relatively inexpensive; and it's easy to install.

After choosing your pattern from an impressive array of colors and textures, you can purchase sheets for do-it-yourself fabrication or order a custom-manufactured unit. If you're making a bar or similar built-in with a sink, consider the advantages of a postformed countertop with an integral backsplash. (Postforming is an industrial process that bends laminate over a curved core by persuading it with heat and pressure.) This kind of countertop comes complete with attached backsplash, ready to install.

If you can't find a laminate pattern you like at the home center, don't despair. Those stores usually display only a fraction of the full possibilities

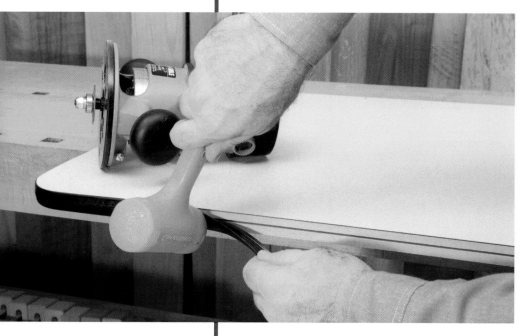

You can purchase plastic laminate in a wide spectrum of colors, textures, and patterns to complement nearly any built-in project.

A postformed countertop comes complete with attached backsplash, ready to install.

Consider the Laminate's Finish

THE REFLECTIVITY OF A laminate surface is an important design consideration. High gloss has a sleek and clean look, but beware of using it on surfaces subject to heavy use because even a tiny scratch is instantly apparent. Toning down the gloss a bit can significantly improve its practicality as a working surface while still displaying a polished look. Many manufacturers produce laminates in several degrees of reflectivity, from a high gloss all the way down to a matte finish. Sometimes you'll find a pattern or color is available in more than one finish, so don't be shy about asking before you make your final choice.

The surface sheen of laminate affects its visual character and also its wear characteristics.

this material offers. Visit laminate manufacturers' websites or seek out a local fabricator who can show you the full array of choices.

You should also be aware that laminate is manufactured in several grades. There's the general-purpose variety, a type made specifically for postforming, and a vertical grade that's not suitable for countertop work. The postforming and vertical grades are typically thinner than their general-purpose counterparts. For extremely demanding environments, you can purchase laminates with high wearing properties or resistance to a wide range of chemicals. Yet one more style of laminate carries the color throughout its thickness, eliminating dark seams at edges.

Tile and stone

Ceramic tiles, or those made from porcelain, glass, or natural stone, make stunningly beautiful counters with extraordinary durability. You can hire a professional to tile your countertop, but the process is also accessible to most do-it-yourselfers. If you choose ceramic tile, make sure you select a floor tile for your countertop. Wall tile simply won't stand up to the rigors of wear experienced by a horizontal application.

Italians, who are considered the world authority on tile, are usually repulsed by the wide grout lines typical of North American installations, rhetorically asking, "Are you interested in having a surface of tile or grout?" If you're looking for a reason other than aesthetics to keep the grout lines slim, consider this—thin lines can mean fewer applications of a water-repellant sealer.

Floor tile and stone are excellent countertop materials that combine beauty and durability.

You can also choose a stone slab for your countertop. It creates an impressive and imposing design statement, but fabricating and installing it means calling in the pros. After your cabinet is in place, the craftsmen will make a full-size template to ensure a perfect fit.

A few words of caution: Just because a countertop is stone doesn't mean you can treat it like dirt. Some stone, such as marble, is relatively soft and can scratch or chip easily. These varieties are also porous, so some spills, such as red wine, can leave a permanent mark. Even seemingly indestructible granite can crack from a sharp blow or the thermal shock of a hot pan. Be sure to consider the maintenance required by the stone you're choosing. Some need periodic sealing of their entire surface.

Concrete

Hearing the words "concrete countertop" can conjure visions of a slab of highway on top of your built-in. In reality, the concrete used for countertops is formed from a mixture that permits fine detail, and a skilled fabricator can make a hardworking surface that's nearly a work of art. The body of the concrete can be dyed before it's poured, or given an aesthetic character-building treatment after it's cured. You can also imbed a wide range of materials into the surface. Seashells, for example, can help the countertop mimic an ancient fossil bed. The inclusion of modern artifacts can transform it into a high-tech sculpture.

Concrete is also a do-it-yourself material. If you want to make your own concrete countertop, you'll find plenty of good books that provide design inspiration, as well as detailed procedures.

Solid-surface materials

There are a number of solid-surface materials on the market, with DuPont's Corian® and

A concrete countertop isn't hard to love. Each one is an original creation built around your needs and ideas.

Wilsonart's Gibraltar® representing two well-known brands. They're made by combining natural materials with resins, and some of the lighter tones posses a translucent quality you may be able to exploit with backlighting.

A number of the patterns bear some resemblance to stone, but it's a distinctly different type of substance, making such comparisons unfair to both materials. You should buy a solid-surface countertop because you like its look and its performance, not to try to fool anyone—including yourself—into believing it's stone.

Although many solid-surface materials machine easily with woodworking tools, you'll probably need to hire a pro for the fabrication. That's because the manufacturers usually restrict sales of the raw material to persons who have completed a factory-approved training program.

Other choices

Beyond the mainstream choices discussed here, still other options exist. Consider brushed stainless steel or a gleaming pattern or texture in another metal, such as copper. Glass offers a wide range: colors from opaque black to crystal clear and textures from gently frosted to deeply pat-

terned. For durability, consider having the glass tempered after fabrication. The process is surprisingly affordable, but it's a one-way street. Once tempered, glass can't be cut or shaped.

Before you choose anything too quirky, though, remember that built-ins typically have a long life span, and countertop removal is not always an easy task.

Making a Laminate Countertop

With a little care, you can make a laminate countertop that rivals one made by an experienced professional. The process starts with the selection of the substrate (base material). Medium density fiberboard will give great results in most applications, but before you make the final choice, check the other choices on p. 26. Adding perimeter strips makes the countertop appear thicker, and if you align them carefully, you'll get crisp corners when you trim the laminate to size. Laminate is adhered with contact cement (don't use any other), which sticks to itself like it was welded. You can't reposition the pieces

Solid-surface materials offer high-tech performance and a myriad of design choices, including inlays and sculpted edge treatments.

once you've assembled them, so you may want to practice some alignment technique before tackling the real thing. As you review the following steps, you'll discover techniques that will help ensure your success.

1. Figure the size of your countertop and cut the ¾-in. substrate to size, as shown in Photo **A**. The typical overhang is 1 in., although you can alter this rule of thumb. See the sidebar "Make a Template," p. 117, for more information. If you're creating scribe allowances as discussed in the next step, however, be sure your substrate begins slightly larger so it will be the correct size after scribing.

2. To make the countertop appear thicker, add 2¼-in.-wide MDF strips around its perimeter. Make sure the strips on all the edges that will be visible after installation lie perfectly flush with the top of the substrate. Glue and nail the strips in place. Where an edge will be scribed to fit against a wavy wall, you can position that strip ¼ in. inboard of the edge, as shown in Photo **B**. That way, you'll be dealing with only a single thickness of material during the fitting process.

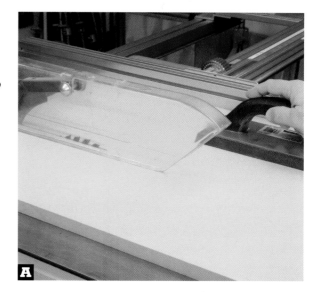

D

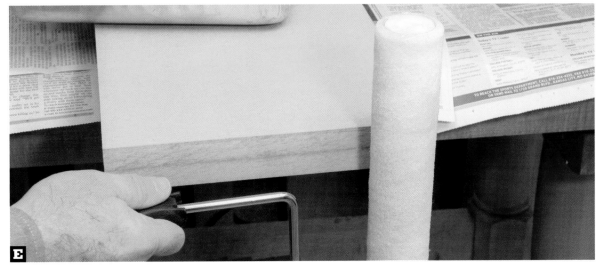

E

Laminate Cutting Guide

WHEN WORKING WITH plastic laminates, this handy addition to your tablesaw's rip fence neatly solves two problems at once. First, the aluminum channel prevents the thin laminate from slipping under your standard fence, which would ruin the cut's accuracy. Secondly the channel's $7/16$-in. depth automatically adds a trimming allowance to the laminate. To use the jig, you simply lock down the fence when the distance from the plywood face to the inner edge of the blade matches the dimension of the substrate. When you guide the laminate in the channel, it emerges $7/16$ in. larger than the fence-to-blade setting.

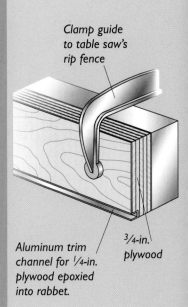

Clamp guide to table saw's rip fence

Aluminum trim channel for $1/4$-in. plywood epoxied into rabbet.

$3/4$-in. plywood

3. If the countertop spans several cabinets, add an intermediate strip, as shown in Photo **C**, wherever a cabinet member can provide support. This will help prevent the countertop from sagging. When you measure for the location of these strips, remember that you're working upside down.

4. Cut the laminate pieces about $7/16$ in. wider and longer than their finished size to provide an allowance for flush trimming. Make the easy cutting jig shown in "Laminate Cutting Guide" at right, to automatically add the trimming

allowance. To minimize chipping, team a sharp blade with a zero-clearance insert and cut the laminate face-up on the tablesaw, as shown in Photo **D**. (See pp. 28 and 77 for more information on zero-clearance inserts and blade selection.)

5. Vacuum or brush away any chips from both the laminate and substrate before applying the contact cement. Follow the manufacturer's recommendations about application technique and tools. A brush is suitable for small areas, but a roller, as shown in Photo **E**, speeds the job.

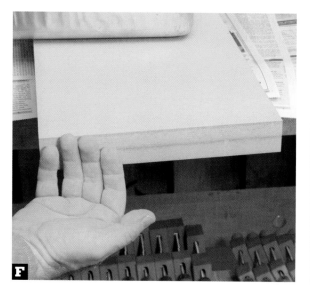

PRO TIP

Begin the banding sequence with the edges that will be least visible after the countertop is installed. This will minimize the appearance of seams.

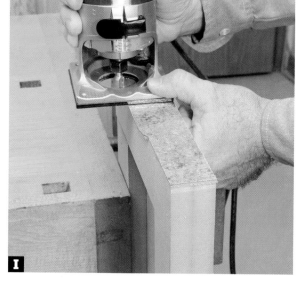

Choose a small trim roller for edges, and switch to a 9-in. roller for large surfaces. When you're banding the edges of the countertop, coat only the edges and the matching pieces of laminate first. You'll deal with the countertop surface after you've installed the banding, as shown in the next steps.

6. Let the contact adhesive dry until it's no longer sticky. Checking with the back of your fingers, as shown in Photo **F**, is a reliable method. Don't wait too long, or you'll exceed the "open time" of the adhesive, which is the window of opportunity for it to bond.

7. The cemented surfaces will grab each other as soon as they touch (that's why they call it contact cement). Keep the laminate separated from the substrate with small dowels, as shown in Photo **G**, while you align the parts, then remove the dowels as you work down the length of the edge.

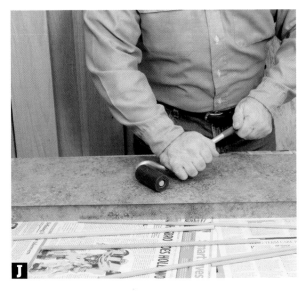

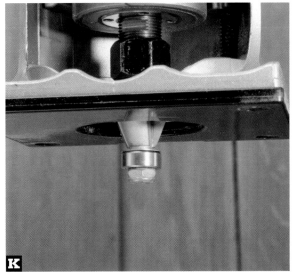

10. After you've banded the edges, scrape any stray adhesive from the uncovered surface of the substrate and apply contact adhesive to it and the laminate for the top. When you adhere the plastic, work from the center outward to avoid trapping air bubbles. Radiate your roller strokes from the center, and grip the tool with both hands to apply maximum pressure, as shown in Photo **J**.

11. Trim away excess laminate with the same technique you used for the banding. After that step, you can switch to a bevel-trimming laminate bit, as shown in the close-up view in Photo **K**, to create a slight chamfer along the edges and corners. Beware of exposing too much of this bit, or you'll risk cutting through the laminate. Your goal is to merely remove most of the sharpness from the edges.

12. As the final step, use a fine-cut file or 150-grit sandpaper in a block to take the edges and corners to final smoothness, as shown in Photo **L**.

8. Press the banding firmly against the substrate. A hard rubber J-roller, such as the one in Photo **H**, helps create a firm bond. Be careful not to tilt the roller along the overhanging edges, or you'll risk cracking the laminate.

9. Using a laminate trimmer with a piloted straight bit, trim away the overhanging laminate, working counterclockwise around the perimeter, as shown in Photo **I**.

Make a Template

MAKE A TEMPLATE WHEN you're dealing with a complex shape or simply want to be absolutely certain your countertop will fit. Plywood ¼ in. thick is an inexpensive material that's easy to cut. For L- or U-shapes or even out-of-square corners, simply butt the plywood pieces together and join them with gussets that span the seams. Drive staples through the plywood into the thicker gussets. Be absolutely certain that you boldly mark the top of the template to avoid the possibility of making the countertop upside down.

Choosing a Laminate Trimmer

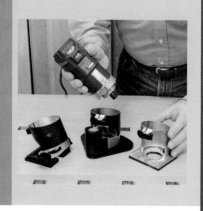

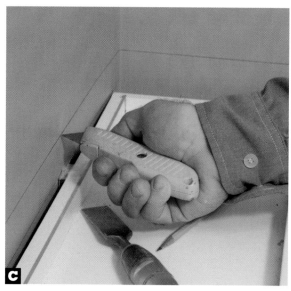

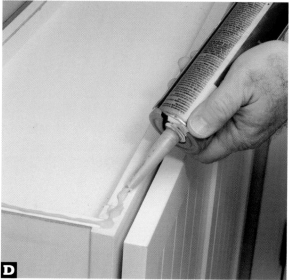

Scribing a countertop

Up until this point, you've taken great care to create a straight countertop. But when it's time to install it, you may discover that the wall at the installation site has more waves than a Hawaiian beach. There are two principal solutions to this problem, and both of them are messy. The first method is to transfer the shape of the wall to the back edge of the counter, then contour the counter to match the wall. The second way requires cutting a shallow recess into the wall and sliding the countertop's edge into it. Choose either method, or try a bit of each. By the way, if your test fitting reveals a gap of no more than ⅛ in. at any point, you don't need to scribe.

1. To scribe the countertop to the wall, position the countertop on top of the cabinet with its rear edge just touching the wall. Make sure the front edge of the countertop is parallel to the cabinet. Select a spacer thick enough to span the gap between the countertop and the wall. As shown in Photo **A**, draw the pencil along the wall to mark the counter. If you're working with a dark laminate, apply masking tape to the back edge of the countertop before scribing the line. You can also use a compass for scribing.

2. Remove the countertop material to the rear of the scribed line. The preferred tool for this operation is a belt sander fitted with a coarse abrasive. A 60-grit belt will cut aggressively, so be careful you don't remove more stock than

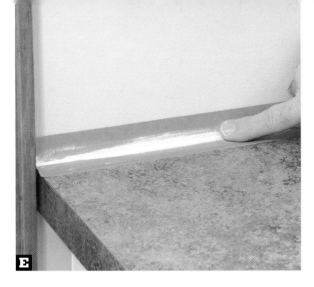

E

F

G

necessary. At the ends of the counter, hold the sander perpendicular to the edge, but along the rest of the line, tilt the sander 5 or 10 degrees from vertical, as shown in Photo **B**. This technique, called back cutting, reduces the contact area to ensure a snug fit. Sand just to the waste side of the line, and test-fit the counter again.

3. If you're working against drywall, you can mark the outline of the counter on the wall and cut through the paper facing with a utility knife, as shown in Photo **C**. A chisel or rotary cutout tool quickly excavates a recess in the gypsum to compensate for a wavy wall. This technique becomes nearly impossible on a hard wall surface such as plaster, so here you'll need to scribe the countertop instead.

4. When you're satisfied with the fit against the wall, adhere the counter to the cabinet by laying down beads of construction adhesive on the top edges of the cabinet, as shown in Photo **D**. Don't go overboard with the adhesive, or you'll simply make a mess. Make certain the edge of the countertop is parallel to the cabinet, and press it down firmly. Alternatively, you can attach the countertop to the carcase with blocks and screws or pockethole screws in the carcase, but exercise extreme care so you don't accidentally puncture the top with a too-long screw.

5. Complete the installation by caulking along the edge. Lay strips of masking tape on the wall and counter, positioning them about ⅛ in. from the wall/counter junction. Lay down a bead of silicone caulk, then create a cove in the bead by lightly smoothing it with a wet fingertip, as shown in Photo **E**.

6. Stripping off the tape removes the excess caulk and reveals the neat joint seen in Photo **F**.

7. As an alternative to the self-edged countertop, consider purchasing a custom-manufactured edge profile. You install it after laminating the top surface. The bevel-edge profile shown in Photo **G** utilizes a single Wilsonart pattern, although you could order contrasting laminate for one or both edges. There are two backing styles: one is smooth, and the other has a ¼-in.-wide projection that registers into a slot cut into the edge of the countertop. Adhere the strips with woodworking glue, and hold them in place with edging clamps or tape until the adhesive sets.

PROTIP

A mechanical pencil in your compass ensures a uniform width of the scribed line. An ordinary wood pencil line becomes wider as the graphite wears.

DESIGN
OPTIONS

◀ ▼ **Laminate takes many edging styles that enhance its appearance. Wood nosing can match your cabinets. Laminated edges mimic solid-surface material. A half-round nosing softens the countertop edge.**

▶ **Wood works equally well as other materials for countertops. This solid maple top is formed from built-up planks edge glued in tabletop fashion and is finished off with bullnosed cherry molding.**

▶ **Varying the height of counter-tops is not a design tool limited to kitchen spaces. Here a lower counter and drawer add visual interest and create the perfect enclave for applying makeup.**

◀ Reminiscent of a French-style cafe, the plank table extends from the counter at the right height for dining chairs. The irregular plank lengths create an integrated addition to this whimsical design.

▼ Different kitchen chores are best done at different heights. The cooking counter should be 2 in. to 3 in. lower than the primary counter, and the baking center even lower to make kneading easier.

HARDWARE

The topic of hardware encompasses several classes of products: from the hardworking "blue collar" nails and screws that hold a project together, to the "white collar" hinges and slides that put doors and drawers in motion, to the "formal dress" set of decorative handles that are one of the style-setters of your built-in. To maintain tranquility–in society as well as in cabinetmaking–you'll be wise to give each class its due respect. If not, your built-in could suffer a range of problems.

You'll want to choose the right fasteners to ensure structural strength. This chapter provides some helpful advice on picking nails and screws that will hold tight in many different materials. Selecting the right hinges and slides will help your built-in deliver the most from every cubic inch of storage space. Finally, picking the right pulls and other visible hardware will make your built-in look right at home. ▶ ▶ ▶

The pencil point in the photo indicates the tiny scale of the entry hole created by a air-powered headless pinner.

Four pneumatic drivers will speed the assembly and installation of your built-in. From left: a finish nailer with an angled magazine for easy access in tight quarters, a brad driver, a narrow-crown stapler, and a headless pinner.

Basic Fasteners

Nails, brads, pins, screws, and staples provide mechanical strength to joints in your built-ins and also attach its hardware and moldings. The novice may feel overwhelmed by all the choices, but a basic understanding of how fasteners achieve their strength will roll back most clouds of confusion. These principles lead to a few rules of thumb about fasteners (see "Rules of Thumb for Fasteners" on the facing page to give you a firm grip on the subject).

The nail and its cousins

When you pinch a nail between your thumb and forefinger, you're mimicking the way the wood grips it after you drive it. The point of the nail splits the wood fibers, which then squeeze back on the shank of the fastener when it's driven. A longer nail has more wood-fiber surface area gripping it, increasing its pull-out resistance. The head of the nail pushes the top board against the target lumber, further strengthening the joint.

Headless pins, as the name implies, don't possess this mechanical advantage, relying solely on the pinning action of the fibers in both pieces of lumber. That's not a serious drawback, though, because you'll typically use headless pins only for light-duty applications—attaching small moldings, for example—where strength isn't an issue.

You'll use hammer-driven and pneumatic (air-powered) finishing nails and brads to join components of your built-in and also to install moldings and other decorative touches. (See p. 35 for more information, including a description of the hammer-driven hard finish nail.)

You'll find headless pins make great fasteners for small-scale moldings because their thin diameter helps prevent splitting. In addition, their tiny entrance hole is virtually invisible, even before you fill it.

A staple has great strength because each leg provides the pinch-grip of a nail, and the leg-spanning wire (called the crown) provides a broad surface that holds the top board firmly in place. The staple is almost always air-driven and excels at tasks where strength is important but its somewhat unsightly appearance remains hidden. A prime example of such an application is the

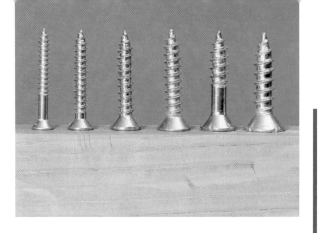

use of staples to attach the plywood back to a cabinet. Woodworkers use narrow-crown staplers much more often than medium- and wide-crown drivers.

How screws work

A screw isn't a threaded nail—it achieves its strength in a completely different manner. For screws, the pressure of the wood fibers against the fastener's shank does not contribute much to its pull-out resistance. Far more important is the surface area of the threads in contact with the wood. To boost the pull-out resistance of a screw, you increase the thread area by choosing a longer screw or one with a larger gauge (diameter), or both. Using a deep-thread screw design (Spax® is one brand) is yet another strategy.

Another consideration when choosing screws is their strength in shear—their ability to resist forces perpendicular to the axis of the screw. Stresses across the axis of a fastener want to bend it—or in a catastrophic failure—shear the screw as if sliced by a bolt cutter. Screws used to hold cabinets to a wall, for example, must have excellent strength in shear.

To increase strength in shear, you want to increase the cross-sectional area of the screw shank. As you'll remember from geometry class,

the area of a circle is pi multiplied by the radius squared. That means that doubling the radius of the fastener increases its cross-sectional area by four times—an enormous boost in strength.

Screws for solid wood and manufactured panels

When you're driving screws into a solid wood target, you'll generally choose a standard thread depth, although a deep thread pattern will produce better holding power in softwoods. The screws for pocket-hole joinery provide a clear example. Pocket-hole screws for hardwood have a fine pitch (distance between threads) and a shallow thread depth. Those for softwoods have a coarser pitch and a deeper thread depth.

When you're working with manufactured panels, choose screws based on the core of the target material rather than its face. For example, it doesn't make any difference whether MDF is topped with melamine, hardwood veneer, or it's a plain MDF panel that you'll paint. When choosing fasteners, treat all of these panels identically.

There are many different types of hardwood plywood cores: veneer, solid wood, composite, particleboard, flakeboard, fiberboard, and MDF. (For more information on these cores, please refer to p. 24.)

Because of this wide variety, it's difficult to give precise recommendations for screws that will give you excellent holding power in all types of plywood. Generally speaking, though, regular wood screws will work well in veneer

SAFETY FIRST

Treat an air nailer with the same respect you would give to a firearm. Never point it anyone, and keep all body parts out of the potential path of the fastener. Be aware that the grain of the wood or knots can radically alter a nail's path, pushing it sideways or even causing it to make a U-turn. Eye protection is mandatory.

Rules of Thumb for Fasteners

CHOOSE FASTENERS with a length at least three times the thickness of the board. For example, drive ¾-in. screws to hold ¼-in. plywood.

Drive fasteners through the thinner piece into the thicker.

Scrap a Phillips driver at the first sign of wear—it will chew up screw heads.

Use screws with fully-threaded shanks (such as sheet-metal screws) when installing hardware.

Base the screw's thread pattern on the target material. For example, cabinet-hanging screws are different for wood and metal studs.

Always drill pilot holes to avoid split lumber and snapped screws.

Don't mix materials when fastening hardware. Putting different metals in contact with each other creates a tiny electrical current that speeds up corrosion.

When driving screws into an MDF or particleboard core, use the lowest clutch setting on your driver that seats the head of the screw. If you spin an overtightened, bottomed-out fastener, it can quickly turn the hole into a bed of powdery fluff with no holding power.

Hole Sizes for Tee-Nuts

Designated Size of Internal Thread	Diameter of Installation Hole (in.)
4-40	11/64
6-62	11/64
8-32	13/64
10-24	15/64
10-32	15/64
1/4-20	5/16
5/16-18	3/8
3/8-16	15/32

Here's an assortment of special screws you'll find helpful (from left): a pocket hole screw for softwood, one for hardwood, the deep-thread Spax design, a Confirmat screw and its special bit.

and lumber core panels. For the other cores, you should consider the Confirmat® screw, which has been specifically engineered to anchor solidly into manufactured panels. Choose the 7-mm by 50-mm Confirmat screw when you're going through ¾-in. stock, and select the 5-mm by 40-mm screw when driving through ½-in. stock. Each size has a special bit that drills the stepped pilot hole for the fastener.

Assembly and Knock-Down Fasteners

Manufacturers have developed a number of specialized fasteners that can simplify the assembly and installation of your built-in projects. For example, knockdown fittings enable you to easily transport cabinet components for on-site assembly instead of lugging fully assembled carcases. Panel connectors allow you to combine separate carcases into a monolithic assembly.

Threaded inserts

The ability to insert machine threads into wooden components means you can assemble the components with the strength of bolts. This

category of fasteners includes tee nuts (which sometimes have prongs for speedy installation) and threaded inserts. For all of these products, the designated size refers to the internal thread.

To install tee nuts, you'll need to drill a hole big enough to accommodate the outside diameter of the fastener shank, as shown in the chart, "Hole Sizes for Tee Nuts" at left.

When working with threaded inserts, choose the external thread style based on whether you're working with solid wood or a manufactured panel. Use the manufacturer's hole-size specification and test the installation in piece of scrap. But don't hesitate to increase the hole size for easier driving, especially in hardwoods.

You may come across threaded inserts with a pronged outer perimeter, but their installation calls for either pressing, which is better suited for industrial machinery, or pounding, which can damage your workpiece. You'll have better success with the thread-in variety.

Knockdown fasteners

If you've ever put together RTA (ready to assemble) furniture or cabinets, you already have experience with knockdown fasteners. Manufacturers

Knockdown corner fittings are easy to install and provide very good joint strength.

rely on industrial equipment to accurately drill holes in a flash, but you can get excellent results in your own shop with careful measurement and a bit of patience. If you're assembling more than a few joints, though, you'll find it's well worth your while to knock together some marking or drilling jigs to speed production.

Cross-dowels combine easy installation with excellent strength. In an upscaled size, this fastener style is brawny enough to produce wobble-free corner joints for a bed frame.

Panel connector bolts are handy for joining together carcase sub-assemblies into a large unit: for an entertainment center or set of bookcases, for example. You'll find these in several different varieties, but the two I like best are called the panel connector and the Chicago bolt (which also goes by the alias "threaded bolt"). Both of these styles span the joint with the female post, providing excellent strength in shear. The panel connector has one specific chore, joining carcases with $\frac{3}{4}$-in.-thick sides. Chicago bolts are more versatile, available in six lengths to help you grip from $^{13}/_{16}$ in. to $2^{9}/_{16}$ in.

Knockdown corner fittings use a cam turned by a screwdriver to pull the joint firmly together. The Julius Blum Company makes this fitting in two sizes: for panels with a thickness of either 16 mm $(^{5}/_{8}$ in.) or 19 mm $(^{3}/_{4}$ in.). You install the nylon press-in fittings into the face of one cabinet piece and drive the special screws centered in the thickness of the other component.

Hinges

Many built-ins will require you to install hinges, and this can be an easy process if you make hinge-selection part of the design process instead of an afterthought.

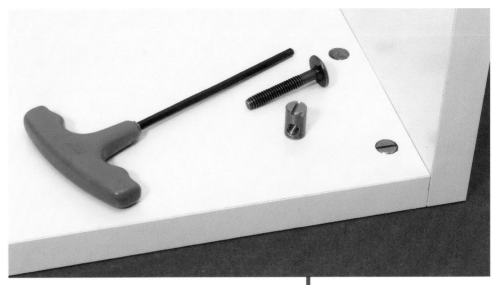

Cross dowels offer excellent strength at right-angle junctions: corners and T-joints. Assembly is fast and wobble-free.

The connector bolt (at top) and Chicago bolt help you join carcase side panels to create large assemblies.

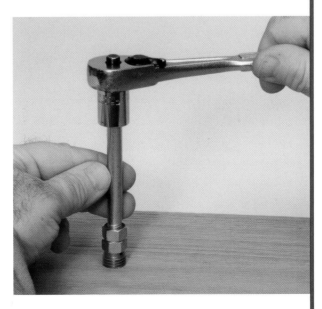

Make an installation tool for threaded inserts from a 4-in. bolt and two nuts.

Install a tee nut flush to the surface by drilling a shallow counterbore before drilling the shank hole.

Here's a line-up of helpful hinges (from left to right): a butt hinge, a no-mortise hinge, a knife hinge, and, at bottom, a surface-mounted hinge.

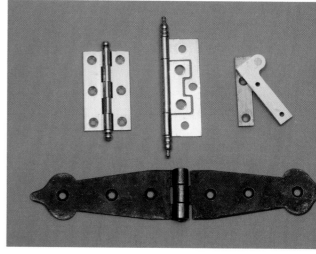

PRO**TIP**

If you mortise a hinge too deeply, raise one leaf with a shim or two. Cereal boxes make great shim stock.

Brass hinge screws are soft and may snap under excessive torque. Eliminate problems by drilling pilot holes and then driving an identical steel screw to cut the threads in the wood. Withdraw it, and install the brass fastener.

One of your primary considerations is what action you want from the hinge: a modest 90-degree opening or a 270-degree arc? Next, you'll need to decide whether you want the hinges to be part of the style statement of your project or if you would prefer discreet or even invisible hinges. Let's take a brief look at some of the major types of hinges, and you can start weighing their attributes and drawbacks.

Surface-mounted hinges

For ease of installation, it's tough to beat surface-mounted hinges. You simply position your door in its opening, mark and drill pilot holes, and drive the screws. There's no tricky mortising, so there's a very short list of things that can go wrong.

Most of the styles associated with surface-mounted hinges are either somewhat rustic or stress the virtues of hand craftsmanship, such as Arts and Crafts. Although strict authenticity would require handmade hardware, that can get expensive very quickly. To conserve your budget, seek out reproductions cast from high-quality originals. Any number of renovation-supply outlets will be happy to send you a catalogue of their wares with your Internet request.

Butt hinges

Butt hinges abound throughout your home: from all of the entry and passage doors to tiny versions that open the lid of a jewelry box. Typical installation involves cutting a mortise in either the frame, the door, or both. You'll find a number of commercial jigs you can use in conjunction with your router to rapidly produce snug-fitting mortises. Of course, if you're a traditionalist, you can cut your mortises with a chisel. But if you're a beginner at hinge installation, practice your mortising skills on scrap stock before cutting into your built-in.

Be absolutely sure you position the center-point of the hinge pin slightly proud (slightly beyond the edge) of the front plane of the carcase and door so it will swing freely. Hinges with decorative finials force this placement, and the additional adornment will enhance your project's statement of style.

Another choice is the no-mortise hinge, which has leaves that fold inside each other. The leaf thickness sets the reveal (open space) at the hinge side of the door. You then carry that same reveal measurement around the other three sides of the perimeter.

Knife hinges are barely visible after installation, a great advantage when you don't want to distract from the cabinetry.

Knife hinges

This hinge style earned its name because its action is similar to that of a jack-knife blade. When the door is closed, only a tiny bit of the hinge shows. For the neatest results, you need to cut the mortises before assembling the carcase, so careful planning is mandatory.

You'll also need to carefully select the hinges from three styles: straight, single-offset, and double-offset. For the offset versions, specify whether you're hinging a right- or left-hand door. The double-offset variety places the center of rotation outside the front plane of the door and cabinet, enabling 270 degrees of rotation. This is great idea for an entertainment center or other application where you want the open door to rest flat against the side of the case.

Euro hinges

Euro hinges were once considered a companion only to melamine-covered cabinets with inset doors. But now you'll find baseplates that adapt these versatile hinges to a wide range of applications, including traditional face-frame designs.

This hinge style has a lot going for it. The hinges are relatively inexpensive, easy to install, and most offer 3-axis adjustability with micrometer precision. You can dial in the exact door placement you want, moving the door up/down, in/out, and side to side.

Euro hinges come in an incredible variety, but you can quickly limit your choices by answering the following questions:

• Is your carcase a face-frame construction or frameless? This answer will help you determine the mounting baseplate for the hinge.

• How far does the door need to swing? Hinges are classified by the maximum angle the mechanism will open a door relative to the front plane of the carcase.

• How does the door fit on the carcase? See "Door Placement Choices" on p. 130 for an explanation of your options.

• What kind of hinge-drilling and installation machinery do you have? The spectrum runs from industrial-grade machinery for high-production output down to low-cost commer-

PRO**TIP**

Euro hinge mechanisms and baseplates aren't interchangeable among the various manufacturers. Stick with one hinge supplier to minimize potential problems.

HERE ARE THREE WAYS
you can place doors on a
carcase: inset, half overlay,
and full overlay. Fitting the
inset style can be the most
demanding because you
must accurately size your
door so its placement results
in an even reveal around its
perimeter.

Euro hinge specification
sheets will give you dimensions for the reveals between
doors that are half and full
overlay.

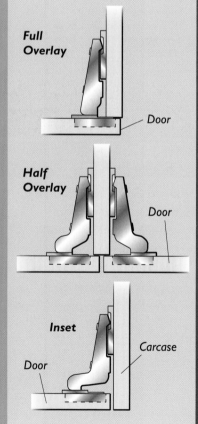

Full Overlay

Door

Half Overlay

Door

Inset

Door

Carcase

cial jigs that start at about the price of a pizza. If you're truly frugal, though, you can get by with a couple of bits and your drill press.

Blumotion is Blum's name for its anti-slam accessory for doors and drawers (see p. 129). You can fit Blumotion pistons on many of Blum's Euro hinges, or choose separate piston fittings to upgrade existing cabinets or another manufactur-er's hinges.

Drawer Slides

The chapter on drawers (p. 86) contains an in-depth discussion of three types of slides I use most often: epoxy-coated, side-mount, and bottom-mounted. In the interest of complete-ness, though, you should know about others.

The first is a manufactured-wood center-mount slide. This is a low-cost classic that's easy to install and will give you dependable service. However, I wouldn't recommend it for drawers that carry a heavy load or that will see heavy use.

There's also a metal center-mounted slide with a ball-bearing mechanism. It glides well, is rated for fairly light duty, but lacks the refine-ments of self-closing or latching.

There's also a drawer slide with two rollers that mount on the face frame and a wheel that rides in a center-mount track. On the plus side, the slide is inexpensive. On the negative side, it's a pain to install, and it's undependable, inaccurate, noisy, flimsy, and highly prone to failure.

Handles and Pulls

Handles, knobs, and pulls must be compatible with the style of your built-in. While that may seem self-evident, it's amazing how often people choose hardware that conflicts with their design.

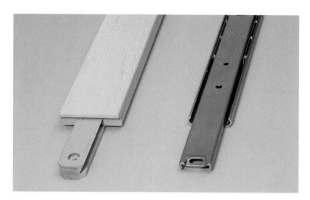

The center-mount wood slide needs just a touch of wax to run slickly. The metal version glides on ball bearings.

To state this another way—simply liking the hardware isn't a good enough reason to choose it. Especially when your built-in emulates furniture and architecture of a specific period, its hardware should be appropriate in shape, material, finish, and method of manufacture to original examples.

Quality hardware isn't inexpensive, but if you economize too much on handles and pulls you risk cheapening the look of your entire built-in.

Don't restrict your hardware search to only metal—wood, ceramic, and glass may be a good companion to your built-in. For example, a con-tinuous wood pull along the end of a melamine door can add both design interest and warmth to the project.

Making your own knobs and pulls provides you with still other options. If your built-in design conveys a modern style, you can give your imagination free rein in both hardware design and materials. For example, both aluminum and brass shape easily with woodworking tools, and so do other materials, such as solid-surface coun-tertop scraps and plastics.

In some cases, you may completely eliminate the need for hardware. For example, drawers concealed behind doors can have a scallop sliced away from the top edge of the drawer front.

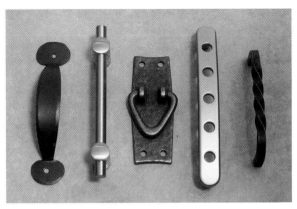

This selection of door-opening hardware hints at the wide spectrum of materials, finishes, and shapes on the market.

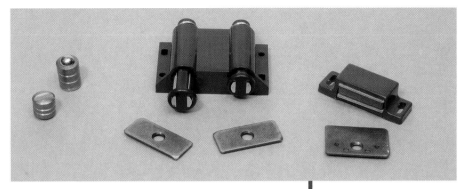

Here are some choices for keeping doors closed: (from left) a bullet catch that installs in the door edge and jamb, a double magnetic touch latch for securing a pair of doors, and a basic magnetic catch.

Miscellaneous Hardware

The design of your built-in may require some specialized hardware to maximize its usefulness. These items may include the following:

• A lid support for a window seat or an overhead bin.

• A drop-front bracket to create a desktop that raises to hide clutter.

• Tracks or rollers for sliding wood or glass doors.

• Wire-management products for an entertainment center or computer workstation.

• Television or audio-component pullouts for an entertainment center.

• Catches, latches, and bolts to keep doors closed.

• Locks to secure items behind doors or inside drawers.

Unfortunately, there's not enough room in this book to describe all of your choices and detail the installation for these products. Fortunately, the Taunton Press offers the *Complete Illustrated Guide to Choosing and Installing Hardware.*

Hardware adds aesthetic details to your built-in. Always match the style of hinges, handles, and pulls to the predominant style of the unit.

WHAT CAN GO WRONG

Avoid powerful magnetic catches (especially rare-earth magnets) near cathode ray tube monitors and televisions, as well as other sensitive electronic gear. The powerful magnetic force fields may interfere with their operation. Magnetically recorded media such as tapes may also be at risk.

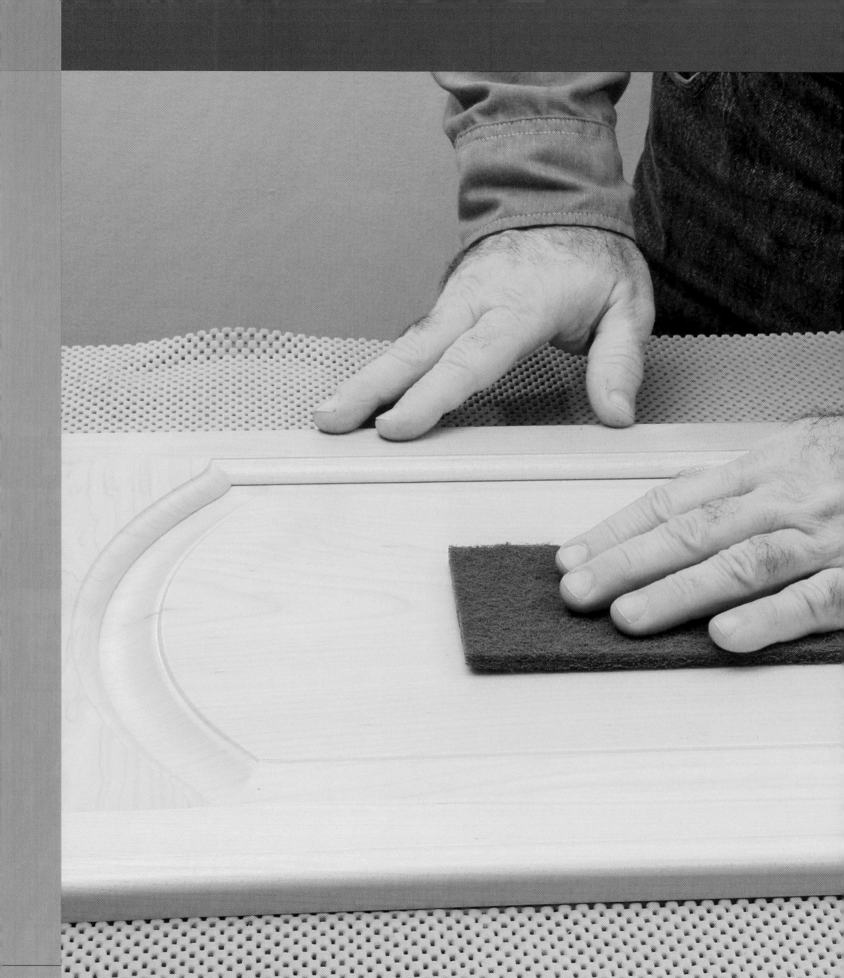

FINISHING

One of the great myths surrounding the finishing process is that it's a mysterious skill similar to alchemy. The truth is that the chemists have done all the hard work, and you really don't need to understand how the molecules link.

Another common misconception is that you must master a wide range of different finishes, including oil, varnish, shellac, lacquer, and a number of different paints. Well, that's simply not true, either. In fact, knowing how to apply paint and a wipe-on clear finish will let you bring nearly any built-in project to a successful conclusion. On the following pages, you'll discover step-by-step photo sequences for both types of finishes.

There's another popular saying that obtaining a good finish is 90 percent about surface preparation. That one is absolutely true, give or take a few percentage points. So this chapter also includes a number of tips and techniques that will help you get your finish off to a smooth start. ▶ ▶ ▶

How Long Should I Sand?

Paint

Some woodworking purists may cringe at the idea of painting one of their creations, but in some cases paint is exactly the right choice. Paint works with a wide range of architectural styles, all the way from traditional to contemporary. In addition, the finish can help your built-in integrate itself more successfully with its surroundings, as if it were part of the original structure, instead of a later addition. In part, that's because paint covers the potential distraction of wood grain and shifts the focus to the overall structure, as well as to molding shapes that assert themselves with crisp shadow lines.

There are also some extremely practical reasons for choosing paint. For one, allows you to considerably reduce the expense of the built-in by using inexpensive manufactured sheets, such as medium density fiberboard (MDF) and economical lumber, such as poplar, instead of costly veneered panels and furniture-grade hardwoods.

Despite the unifying appearance paint creates on dissimilar surfaces, however, you can't let

Improvise a curved sanding block to conform to concave shapes. You can easily shape foam packing material to match moldings.

material choice be an afterthought. For example, oak will prove a poor choice under paint because its open grain structure will show through the finish.

A second practical factor recommending paint is the fact that it's easier for a beginner—both in woodworking and in finishing—to achieve a high-quality result. An imprecise joint that would appear glaringly obvious under a clear coat disappears thanks to wood putty and the opacity of the paint. Paint also allows you to easily conceal problems that can show up during the finishing process. For example, if scratches appear after you've applied the first coat of primer, it's no big deal. But the same scratches after a stain application pose a serious problem. Of course, choosing a painted finish doesn't issue you a license for slipshod workmanship; it simply means you can more easily repair and conceal mistakes.

Sanding curves

When sanding curves, such as those in crown molding, back up your abrasive with something moderately rigid. Try a manufactured block, a dowel, a short length of rubber hose, a small mailing tube, or something you find around your home or shop. The backing will help the abrasive conform to the curve, smoothing it more quickly and evenly. Trying to work with fingertip pressure alone is tiring and inefficient, and can turn out a surface that's smooth but uneven.

Applying a painted finish

1. Power sanding takes a lot of the drudgery out of the chore, but you should always hand-sand the last pass. I prefer the hard rubber block shown in Photo **A**, which you can purchase from an auto-body finishing supplier. Sanding to 120- or 150-grit is plenty.

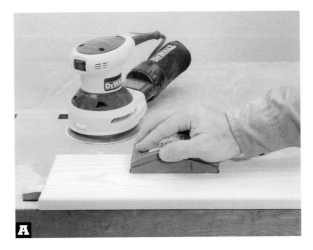

A

B

C

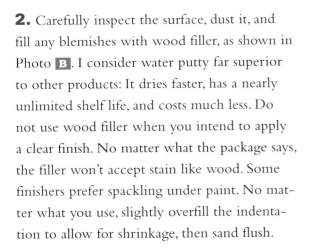

D

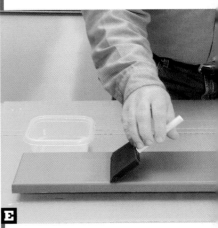

E

2. Carefully inspect the surface, dust it, and fill any blemishes with wood filler, as shown in Photo **B**. I consider water putty far superior to other products: It dries faster, has a nearly unlimited shelf life, and costs much less. Do not use wood filler when you intend to apply a clear finish. No matter what the package says, the filler won't accept stain like wood. Some finishers prefer spackling under paint. No matter what you use, slightly overfill the indentation to allow for shrinkage, then sand flush.

3. Dust or vacuum the surface after sanding any filler and apply a coat of primer compatible with your color coat. Since we're using a latex-based paint here, a 100 percent acrylic primer is appropriate, as shown in Photo **C**. It also reduces the level of fumes and enables soap-and-water cleanup. After the primer dries, sand lightly to level the primer. If any imperfections come to light, spot-prime them, then reprime the entire project. Sand again and remove the dust.

4. Apply the first color coat, as shown in Photo **D**. Choose an enamel because it will produce a smooth hard surface. Don't try to achieve one-coat coverage—that will encour-

age you to slather on the paint too thickly. Add a conditioner called Floetrol® to latex paint to improve flow-out and minimize brush marks. (For oil-based paint, use Penetrol®.) Spread the paint evenly, but don't over-brush it. After the first coat dries, lightly sand to smooth the surface and raise a "tooth" for the second coat; then remove the dust and apply a second coat.

5. At this point, you can consider the paint job finished or you can add a clear coat, as shown in Photo **E**. This final step protects the paint, gives its color greater depth, and can even out its surface sheen. To avoid possible color shifts, choose a clear-coat product that won't yellow with age. Water-based polyurethane is an excellent choice. Make sure this clear coat is com-

WHAT CAN GO WRONG

"Breaking the corners" means softening the edges slightly with light sanding. Don't overdo it, though, or you'll ruin the crispness of your lines. Breaking the corners improves finish adhesion because liquids tend to flow away from sharp junctions, and that could compromise the integrity of paint and film-building clear finishes.

SAFETY FIRST

Stains and dyes can be extremely long-lasting on skin. But appearance isn't the only reason to wear gloves during the application process. Your skin can absorb solvents as well as the chemicals in the pigments. Disposable gloves provide an inexpensive insurance against these hazards. Choose vinyl gloves if you're allergic to latex.

patible with your paint by testing it on a piece of painted scrap material.

Stains, Dyes, and Clear Finishes

At its most basic level, a clear finish protects the wood from dirt and oil. In addition, the finishing procedure brings out the beauty of the wood itself. As you'll see, choosing the right finish produces a surface that meets both the durability and aesthetic requirements of your built-in.

The careful use of stains and dyes can also enhance the wood's character, but you'll want to be careful not to expect more from these materials than they can deliver.

Stains and dyes

Before we get too far into the topic of stains and dyes, I'd like to dispose of a prevalent misconception. Some novices feel they can build a project from any wood that's cheap and available, slap on a cherry stain, and magically obtain a flawless duplicate of cherry wood. If you want your proj-

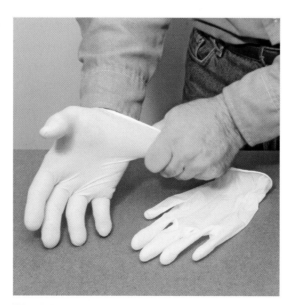

Vinyl, latex, or nitrile gloves provide better dexterity than bulky rubber gloves.

ect to look like cherry, build it from cherry. Then you can use a stain or dye to slightly modify the tone to suit your taste.

Both stains and dyes are colorants, but they work in different ways. Stains use relatively large pigment particles suspended in a solvent (usually petroleum based). When you wipe on the stain, it colors all of the wood, but the particles can settle in pores, sanding scratches, and other blemishes, emphasizing them.

Dyes are pigments ground so finely they completely dissolve in their solvent—water, oil, or alcohol. Water-soluble dyes can tint water-borne finishes, and you can mix oil-soluble dyes into oil-based varnishes and other finishes.

Certain soft- and hardwoods, like cherry, birch, and maple, accept stains unevenly, producing unsightly blotches. Unfortunately, you rarely know if a wood is going to blotch until after you've applied the stain. To be safe, conduct a test on scrap lumber. Applying a pre-stain wood conditioner can help prevent or at least minimize the problem, but conditioners also lighten the tone of the stain.

Dyes aren't a foolproof antidote to blotchiness. In this case, the preventative treatment is a coat of sizing. Make your own by mixing one part (by weight) of granular hide glue with nine parts of drinking-quality water. Spread a thin coat of size, and let it dry before you dye.

Alcohol-based dyes dry very rapidly, so for large surfaces, spraying is virtually the only application that won't leave lap marks. You can flow on water- and oil-based dyes with a brush or rag. Dyes work quickly, so leaving the surface wet for a while won't change the tone. Stains are more time sensitive, so you need to work at a consistent pace, applying, then wiping up the excess. A second coat of stain can deepen the tone.

Clear Finishes

Here's a quick look at the lineup of clear finishes. Each product has advantages and drawbacks, so match the finish to the application method you prefer, your skill level, and the requirements of your project.

Oil finishes This category includes "pure" oils, such as boiled linseed oil, tung oil, mineral oil, walnut oil, and others with no dryers. The oils may be clear or contain colorants.

To apply such an oil finish, you simply flood the surface of your project, let the oil soak in, and wipe away the excess with cloths. Although each application is fast and easy, oils without dryers can take a long time to cure: Allowing at least a week between coats may be necessary. A single coat is seldom adequate, so you may find yourself applying four to six coats before the wood stops absorbing the oil.

Oils don't contain solids that build a surface film, so they are considered "close to the wood"

You have a wide range of choices among clear finishes, from barely-there oil to hard-wearing coatings.

finishes. The lack of a protective film means the wood scratches easily, but you can quickly renew an oil finish by simply cleaning the surface and laying on another coat. A coat of wax gives the durability of the finish a modest boost.

Choosing Brushes

A QUALITY BRUSH SERVES AS YOUR PAINTING partner, helping you lay down a smooth and even coat. Don't handicap yourself by trying to save a few dollars with a cheap brush. A nylon brush with flagged (split) bristle ends is a quality tool, and you'll also find excellent brushes with a blend of nylon and polyester bristles. Brushes with only polyester bristles are usually considered inferior.

Some synthetic bristles will work well with either oil-based or water-borne finishes, but many finishers consider natural-bristle brushes as the top of the line for oil-based paints and clear coats. For laying down a smooth varnish, the pros choose a badger brush.

An angled sash brush permits you to easily reach into corners. A 2-in. or 2½-in. brush works well for general use, but for intricate moldings you may want to go down to a 1½-in. sash brush.

For flat surfaces, a 3-in. square brush will speed your work and still be easy to control.

Don't skimp on quality when choosing brushes. They are an investment that will lay down smooth finishes for years.

WHAT CAN GO WRONG

No matter how well you clean your brushes, small amounts of the finish can remain and possibly contaminate the next application. Even if you use synthetic brushes suited for both oil- and water-based finishes, minimize problems by keeping one set of brushes for oil-based primers and paint, and another group for water-borne products. Even when the solvent is compatible, don't use the same brush for paint and clear coats, or you could risk a cloudy appearance.

WHAT CAN GO WRONG

Whenever you test stains and dyes, conduct your experiments on wood you've sanded to the same smoothness as your project. Wood that's rougher accepts color differently, and sanding can burnish the surface, inhibiting the absorption of the liquid. In addition, you should let the surface dry and apply at least one coat of clear finish before giving the color your final approval. By the way, write notes on your sample boards so you don't need to trust your memory.

Oil/varnish blends Oil/varnish products combine an oil finish with varnish, which contains one or more chemical dryers. Watco® Danish Oil Finish is an example of such a finish. Application of these blends entails the identical steps for an oil finish: flood the surface, wait, wipe off the excess. These finishes exhibit most of the attributes of pure oil finishes, but the dryers reduce the wait time between coats. Not a film-building finish, it's low on durability but easy to repair. Some contain colorants, allowing you to bypass a separate staining.

Varnish This category encompasses a wide range of film-building products, from thick gels to water-thin formulations. You'll find products you can wipe on, spray on, or brush. Some are crystal clear, others cover a wide spectrum from a faint amber to intense colorants that eliminate staining.

You'll find both petroleum- and water-based varnishes, and both produce finishes that can stand up to abrasion and occasional spills. Polyurethane formulations are technically chemically different from traditional varnishes, but their application and results are similar, so we'll consider them part of this category.

For most built-in projects, varnish combines relatively easy application with durable results.

Shellac Shellac is a versatile and fast-drying film-building finish, but water, alcohol, heat, and most strong household cleaners can easily damage it. As a result, it's a poor choice for a countertop, but good for many vertical surfaces. You can mix shellac flakes with denatured alcohol, or purchase premixed shellac in liquid or aerosol forms. Liquid shellac ages to a point where it won't cure when applied, so be sure to check the expiration date on the container.

There are several tones of shellac, from nearly clear blond to a tone called orange, though it's actually more of an amber shade.

Shellac is often employed under other finishes because it seals the wood and dries quickly. Applying shellac to the end grain of wood can inhibit stain penetration so these surfaces don't turn excessively dark by sucking up stain.

Lacquer Lacquer is a popular production finish because it dries rapidly, permitting you to apply a number of coats within a single day. The fast drying speed also gives airborne dust less time to settle on the wet surface and create tiny bumps called nibs. It's also a relatively easy finish to repair because a fresh coat partially dissolves the existing film to unite with it.

Lacquer is moderately durable, although standing water and other spills can lift the finish. You can apply lacquer with a high-quality brush if you maintain a wet edge and avoid working over areas that have started to set, but spraying is the most efficient application method.

Spraying allows you to cover areas quickly. Aerosol cans are adequate for small projects, but large-scale projects require a spray-gun setup. Achieving a good spray finish requires practice,

Getting the Right Gloss

ACHIEVING A FLAWLESS GLOSSY finish is extremely difficult because the highly reflective surface highlights even tiny imperfections. That's why most people opt for a reduced sheen, such as satin. The scale of glossiness goes by various names among paint and finish manufacturers. You'll see terms such as semigloss, eggshell, satin, and others.

Manufacturers generally modify the sheen by suspending fine particles of silica in the finish, which disperse the light. That works well with paints, but these tiny specks can give clear finishes a cloudy appearance when you apply more than one coat. When you want a satin sheen with a clear finish, one or two coats of a clear gloss will start to build the film thickness you need for protection without obscuring the natural beauty of the wood. You can then apply a single coat of satin finish to obtain the sheen you want.

so set aside some time and hone your skills on scrap materials before tackling your project. Compared to old-fashioned guns, spray guns using a technology called HVLP (high volume low pressure) deliver more finish onto your project instead of wasting it as overspray. You'll find HVLP spray systems powered by a turbine system or by a conventional air compressor.

Specialty finishes and other strategies

Furniture factories and some cabinet shops use specialty coatings such as catalyzed finishes to provide extremely durable surfaces that will give long service even in environments as demanding as a kitchen or laundry room. However, you may find it impossible to purchase these finishes in less than industrial volumes. In addition, the finish may require specialized application equipment, as well as demanding safety precautions.

So if you want an ultra-durable finish—or simply want to skip all the time and work associated with application—contact local cabinetmakers to get pricing on subcontracting this part of your project.

Wipe-on Finishes

1. Sand the wood to final smoothness (150-grit is usually sufficient), and ease the edges and corners. As shown in Photo **A**, use a sanding block whenever possible to help ensure flat surfaces. If the project has small holes, such as those made by brads attaching molding, do not fill them at this time.

2. Dust or vacuum the project, then wipe the surfaces with a cloth slightly dampened with naphtha or mineral spirits, as shown in Photo **B**. This step lifts dust from the wood's pores and also lets you see sanding scratches or other defects that require more work. Take care of those problems before moving to the next step.

3. Shake or stir the finish to ensure it's evenly blended. Pour the liquid through a paint filter to remove any impurities. The wire stand holding the filter funnel in Photo **C** is an inexpensive convenience. A shallow kitchen storage container provides easy access for the applicator cloth and has a snap-on lid that will keep the finish fresh for a day or two.

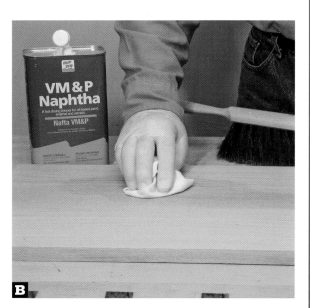

Some petroleum-based products generate heat as they dry, and under certain conditions rags soaked with these volatile solvents can burst into flames in a process known as spontaneous combustion. To kill this hazard, either drown or hang the rags. By drowning, I mean thoroughly wetting the rags under running water.

Hanging means clipping the rags to a clothesline outdoors or in a similarly well-ventilated area. To be doubly sure you've eliminated the hazard, you can drown the rags before hanging them. When the rags are dry, you can safely toss them in the trash can.

You can temporarily store solvent-soaked rags in an approved safety container with a tightly fitting lid, but you must empty the can daily.

4. Cut cloths from soft white cotton fabric— old T-shirts are ideal. Shake the cloths to remove loose threads from the cut edges and fold the edges inward to form an application pad. Wearing gloves to protect your hands, dip the pad to charge it with finish, and gently squeeze it so it doesn't drip. Photo **D** shows how you glide the pad over the wood to spread the finish. Inspect the surface by looking at it toward a light placed at a low angle. The reflection quickly reveals dry areas. Repeat the dip-and-glide procedure, working from a wet edge toward dry areas until you've covered all the surfaces. Your goal is to apply smooth thin coats that will dry quickly. Trying to build a thick film with a heavy coat will extend the drying time and can lead to runs, sags, and other problems

5. When the finish dries, sand the surface very lightly with 220-grit sandpaper, as shown in Photo **E**. Your goal is to simply remove dust particles that settled into the finish when it was wet and to give this coat a tooth to improve

the adhesion of the second coat. If your inspection reveals any sags or runs, sand to flatten the surface. Dust or vacuum the surface, and then lightly dust it with a tack cloth to lift away any remaining dust.

This type of finish utilizes thin applications, so three coats is the minimum I apply. For more durability, go to a fourth coat. Each layer is fast and easy, so it's not really a lot of work.

6. Before you apply the final coat of finish, fill in any brad holes that resulted from attaching the moldings. Purchase several jars of color putty: one that's a close match for most of the wood, and one each that are lighter and darker than the overall tone. Take a dab of each color, and mix them into a streaky ball. Rub the ball over a nail hole to fill it, as shown in Photo **F**, using a portion of the putty that's close in tone to the wood at that location. Generally, a putty tone that's slightly lighter than the wood will be far less noticeable than one that's darker. If

Tack Cloth Defeats Dust

TRAPPED DUST CAN RUIN THE APPEARANCE OF ANY finish, and even the cleanest work area isn't surgically pure. The professional finisher's secret weapon is a tack cloth, which is merely a piece of cheesecloth made sticky with a small amount of uncured varnish. Tack cloths are packed flat at the paint store, but after you open the packaging completely unfold the cloth, then gently crumple it. Dust your project with a light touch—don't scrub the surface. Store the cloth in zip-top plastic bag to keep it clean and fresh between uses.

Even when you use a light touch, the cloth can transfer a small amount of its varnish to the surface. That's why you shouldn't utilize a tack cloth when you're applying a water-borne finish. In that case, substitute a clean cotton cloth barely dampened with water.

Lift dust with a tack cloth before applying each coat of finish.

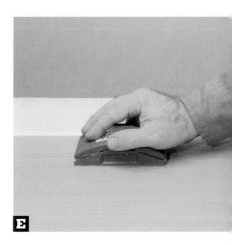

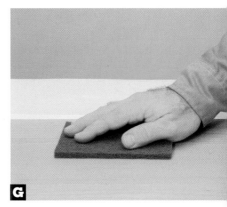

you don't get it right on the first try, just rub the ball on the wood again to transfer a different tone.

7. When the final coat of finish is dry, you can fine-tune its reflectivity by gently rubbing the surface with fine steel wool or a flexible abrasive pad, as shown in Photo **G**. After the finish has cured for a month, applying a couple of coats of paste wax is the final step. Woodworking specialty suppliers offer a selection of waxes, including tinted varieties that conceal scratches. Although I've used several of these, I usually get a good quality paste wax from the local auto-parts store. Avoid products marked as a cleaner/wax because these contain abrasives that can scour away part of your finish.

True Grit

THE WORLDWIDE DISTRIBUTION of woodworking products means that references to sandpaper grits are not as simple as they used to be. In fact, you may encounter six or more different grading systems. But before you despair that this is a hopelessly complicated situation, you can take comfort that two systems dominate in North America, and their grit designations are quite close to each other in the woodworking range.

If your coated abrasives originated on the European continent, they probably follow the system of the Federation of European Producers of Abrasives (FEPA). A prefix of P before the grit number—P150, for example—identifies products of this system.

If there's no prefix, the product probably originated in North America and belongs to the system of the Coated Abrasives Manufacturers Institute (CAMI). Numbers in the CAMI and FEPA systems closely parallel each other up to approximately 220-grit, and then numbers designating finer grits in the FEPA system accelerate more rapidly.

Some people prefer FEPA-graded products because they feel that they produce more consistent results. To bolster that contention, they cite the fact that the FEPA system specifies a tighter tolerance range for particles in each grit designation.

MEDIA CENTERS

Some people who are old enough to start forgetting a lot of other things still have clear memories of the family's television set. But even if those recollections are sharp, the picture sure wasn't–no matter how you adjusted the "rabbit ears" or even if you added a small potato or a crumple of aluminum foil to each of the antenna stalks. Then color came to television, transforming the grainy black-and-white image into a fuzzy color picture.

As technology advanced, picture quality improved and colors became more natural. In recent years, there's been a quantum leap in screen size, and sound systems for the home can closely recreate the theater experience.

As a result, many people are investing their entertainment dollars into their home and installing built-ins to house their valuable equipment. The following chapter shows the steps involved in creating a home-theater or entertainment center from scratch. You'll pick up design tips, learn construction strategies, and discover installation secrets. ▶ ▶ ▶

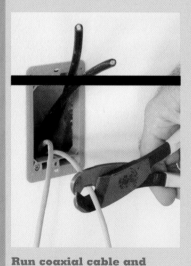

Run coaxial cable and other low-voltage wires to a backless wall box. Keep separate from power wires.

Planning

An entertainment center design is complicated by its purpose. It must accommodate the screen, speakers, and media players—plus the "chases" that carry the wiring between components.

The installation shown here consists of five major components: four carcases and a base. The center unit accounts for two of the carcases. The lower one features two drawers for media storage and two doors with grill-cloth inserts. The center channel speaker resides behind one door, and the other door conceals the subwoofer. The upper carcase encloses the flat panel monitor, and a generous shelf above holds display items. These carcases project 6 in. into the room beyond the flanking units to add variety to the design.

The side carcases are 3 in. narrower than their face frames, a design element with three important benefits. First, it minimizes the area of contact with the center carcases and side walls, reducing alignment problems. Second, it creates a series of vertical wire chases. (To make horizontal cable paths, I drilled holes though the lower side edges of these carcases and the lower central one.) Third, the vent hole drilled through the tuner and media-gear compartment lets heat escape up the wire chase, which acts like a chimney, keeping the equipment cool.

The side carcases hold additional drawers, open display shelves, and doors that conceal electronic equipment and other items. The doors with grill-cloth inserts hide the front side channel speakers and provide plenty of room to adjust their position for optimum enjoyment.

Survey the site

When you're going to build a large-scale project—especially one that will run between two walls—your first step is to survey the site to find the point on the main installation surface that projects furthest into the room. Then you can plan the installation so that all the cabinet backs are even with a vertical plane at this point.

COMPONENTS OF AN ENTERTAINMENT CENTER

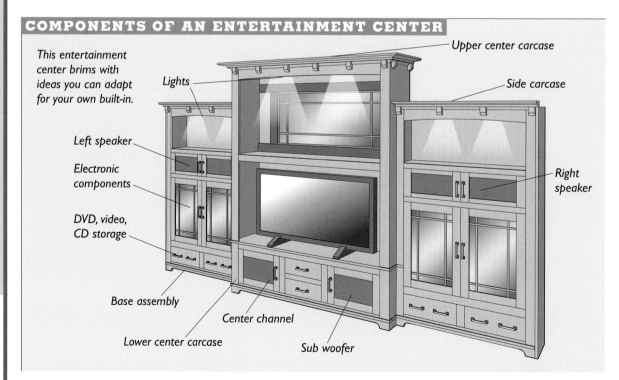

This entertainment center brims with ideas you can adapt for your own built-in.

Lights — Upper center carcase — Side carcase — Left speaker — Electronic components — DVD, video, CD storage — Right speaker — Base assembly — Center channel — Lower center carcase — Sub woofer

A

B

1. For starters, hold a straightedge horizontally along the wall, as shown in Photo **A**. This will quickly identify the locations of hills and valleys. Slide the straightedge over the entire surface to make sure you identify any potential problem areas. Unless there are some severely bowed studs, it isn't necessary to repair the wall—simply mark the high areas with a pencil or a piece of masking tape.

2. Next, go over the wall with a 6-ft. level held vertically, as shown in Photo **B**. If you don't want to invest in a long level, you can team up a short level with a straightedge, such as a piece of 1x4 lumber. This procedure will quickly reveal whether the overall plane of the wall tilts

forward, backward, or is actually plumb. Finally, go over the high marks you made earlier and you'll identify the furthest projection into the room. This identifies the rear installation plane for your built-ins.

In this installation, the units rest on a platform, so its rear edge cannot be any further back than the plane I just identified. To be on the safe side, I moved that edge an additional ¼ in. forward.

Build the Carcases

A few fortunate woodworkers have cavernous shops equipped with a tablesaw with side extensions and an outfeed table the size of a small aircraft landing strip. Such a setup makes easy work of slicing full plywood sheets. The rest of us need another way to break sheet goods into manageable pieces (see "Cutting Large Stock," on p. 146).

1. After you've sliced the components to size, cut the dadoes and rabbets into the sides. This is an operation you can perform with a dado head in your tablesaw, but jumbo-size pieces can quickly turn the process into an awkward wrestling match. An easy alternative is to clamp two

A

TRADE SECRET

As a general rule, the best side of the plywood will face the inside of a carcase. That's because the outer surfaces of end panels are generally hidden from view. If you need to show a finished end panel, cover it with a ¼-in. plywood skin, following the procedure shown on p. 161. This is easy to do when you build a face frame that overhangs the side, as shown on p. 81.

sides with their back edges touching, as shown in Photo **A** on p. 145. You can then use a guide clamp and baseplate (the system shown is from Tru-Grip®) to guide your router. Several manufacturers make router bits that cut dadoes that are a close match for the actual thickness of plywood panels. For example, the CMT bit I used cuts a $^{23}/_{32}$-in. dado, usually a great fit for nominal $^{3}/_{4}$-in. plywood.

2. Before assembling the carcases, create pathways for the wiring. As shown in Photo **B**,

B

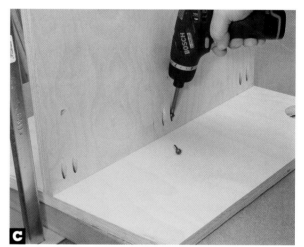

C

I used a 2½-in. hole saw to match a standard grommet size. The generously sized holes also make it easy to fish cables throughout the built-in.

3. To keep the carcase joinery as simple as possible, I relied on pocket hole screws where they would be hidden from view. For example, the partitions in the center base unit were an excellent candidate for this easy method, as shown in Photo **C**. The remainder of the carcase joinery involved basic gluing, clamping, and screwing. To avoid twisting, assemble the carcase on a flat surface. Cut the backs to size and set them aside for now.

Cutting Large Stock

FOLLOWING A LINE freehand with a circular saw is fast, but won't provide the accuracy required for cabinet construction. But you can cut the stock slightly oversized, then trim it at the tablesaw.

A quality saw guide lets you skip that second step, however, slashing time and effort. Some systems, such as the Tru-Grip clamp shown top right let you mount your saw to a base that registers with a channel along the guide to prevent the blade from wandering. Make your first cut in scrap to determine how far to offset the guide from the cutline.

The Festool® system shown bottom right engineers a channel right into the saw's shoe, so you place the edge of the guiderail right on the cutline. That makes it faster and easier to use, but gaining that convenience requires a substantial investment.

After you've assembled the face frame, turn it over to inspect the joints. Most times, they will need only a light sanding. For more serious alignment issues, a cabinet scraper removes thin shavings, quickly solving the problem.

Apply finish, then assemble

At this point, you've made the plywood carcase, the face frame, and the back. Completing the assembly creates corners that are difficult to reach, so I prefer to stain and apply the finish first.

Plywood and solid lumber often react differently to stains, so it's a good idea to conduct tests on scraps sanded to the final smoothness of the project. In this case, the differences were so dramatic I had to conduct a number of experiments to get the plywood to match the lumber (see "Conducting Stain Tests" on p. 149).

After you've stained the pieces, apply a clear finish. I used a rag to glide on a wipe-on polyurethane. For more about finishing, see p. 132.

4. Now you can direct your attention to making the face frames. Carefully check the dimensions of the parts against the completed carcases. In this entertainment center, each of the three main units has a curved top rail. Photo **D** shows how a template and a flush trim bit in the router table produces a completed part fast. For more on pattern routing, see "Pattern Routing Speeds Production" at right.

5. Assemble the face frames with pocket hole screws. If the piece is wide enough, as shown in Photo **E**, you can use two of the locking grip face clamps designed for this purpose. Be sure that you center the large pad of the clamp over the joint line on the visible face.

Pattern Routing Speeds Production

I've never hesitated to make a router pattern when a project required multiple parts. But for a long time, I thought that the pattern wasn't worth the effort for only a single piece. Then one day—in the middle of sanding a curved rail—it dawned on me that smoothing a ¼-in. plywood template would have been much easier than shaping triple that thickness in white oak. From then on, I've always relied on pattern-routing to make curved parts. Use a sharp bit, and the completed piece will require only minimal sanding.

WHAT CAN GO WRONG

You can save some money by choosing a secondary species of plywood, such as birch, for the parts of your built-in that won't be visible. But that material may not be identical in thickness to the primary plywood, and that can complicate the joinery. For example, cutting dadoes in two different widths will involve extra time for tool setup, and you'll need to be extremely careful to avoid mistakes. In the end, saving some cash may cost you more time than it's worth.

A

B

1. Put the carcase face down on a flat surface, and square it with equal diagonals. Attach the back with air-driven staples or brads, as shown in Photo **A**. The chalk lines mark the intermediate shelves and dividers.

2. Drill the carcase for the pocket hole screws that will attach the face-frame. The outside faces of the side carcases will be hidden after installation, so that's where I drilled, as shown in Photo **B**. I left the face-frame off the top center unit, preferring to position it when the carcase was in its final location.

Build a Solid Base

Before you start building the base, confirm its dimensions by double-checking the finished size of the carcases.

1. An air nailer is a quick way to assemble the ladder-type base, as shown in Photo **A**.

2. Temporarily position the base at the installation site and lay masking tape to define its perimeter. Depending on the tools you have available, you'll choose one of two methods to find the high point within the base's footprint. With regular spirit levels, follow the procedure shown on pp. 159–160. But if you have a rotary head laser level, set it up, as shown in Photo **B**. Holding a yardstick vertically, put its end against the floor at a variety of spots within the taped area. The actual measurement on the stick doesn't matter—you're simply looking for the spot that produces the smallest measurement because that indicates the high spot on the floor. By the way, the red glasses I'm wearing in the photo are not a fashion statement. Instead, they are a laser accessory that allows you to see the beam more clearly.

3. Now you can replace the platform and shim it level front to back as well as side to side. Using regular spirit levels for this part of the operation, as shown in Photo **C**, is easy and dependable. Ensure that the platform rests on the high spot of the floor you identified earlier (place a weight there, if necessary), and position all your shims.

4. Insert shims, if needed, between the wall and the back edge of the platform. Double-check the position of the platform to ensure that it's in the right place. Drill pilot holes, then drive screws into the studs, as shown in Photo **D**, making sure that the platform doesn't shift. To get the final height needed for the platform, you can nail on strips of plywood.

A

B

C

D

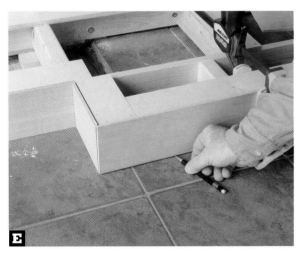

E

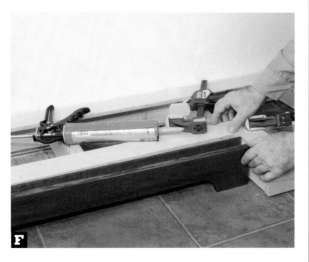

F

Conducting Stain Tests

TO TEST STAIN MIXTURES, label test boards with the proportions of the mixtures and stir the sample thoroughly before applying it. The tone will change as it dries—accelerate the process with a hair dryer.

Here are the final results, using General Finishes® gel stains. For the solid wood, I liked equal parts Java and Georgian Cherry. But this turned too red on the plywood, so my first test was Java alone. This produced a tone that needed yellow, so I got some Nutmeg stain and experimented with the proportions. In the end, the plywood stain was 4 parts Nutmeg to 1 part Java.

5. If the floor is uneven, you'll need to scribe the lower edge of the plywood backing boards to ensure a snug fit, as shown in Photo **E**. Bandsaw just to the waste side of the line, then file or sand to the line.

6. After cutting the feet to shape, stain and fin-ish all the parts before installation. Then install them with construction adhesive and clamps, as shown in Photo **F**. You can also shoot finish-ing nails in areas that will later be covered by another molding strip.

Install the Cabinets

1. Set the center base cabinet into place, carefully aligning it. I planned the face frame to overhang the front of the footed base by 1/16-in. A sample of plastic laminate is a handy gauge to verify this reveal, as shown in Photo **A**. Insert shims between the back of the cabinet and the wall, then screw it in place. Verify that this doesn't move the cabinet.

2. Stack the top center carcase in place and it check its alignment, as shown in Photo **B**. Drive screws upward through the bottom cabinet to hold it in place, but don't fasten it to the wall yet.

3. Now you'll turn your attention to the side cabinets. Where these meet the wall, I settled on a type of reverse reveal, as shown in "The Reveal Assembly," on the facing page. Install the finished assembly at each wall, as shown in Photo **C**.

4. Set one of the side cabinets into place, butting the back of the face-frame against the reveal assembly and the edge of its face-frame against the center cabinets. Check the reveal at the bottom of the cabinet as well for plumb. When you're satisfied with the fit, run a strip of masking tape where the face-frame meets the center cabinets, as shown in Photo **D**.

5. Jockey the side cabinet far enough out of the way to mark a series of screws you'll drive through the center cabinet into the edge of the face-frame of the side cabinet. Mark the centers of the holes 3/8 in. from the edge of the tape and drill pilot holes, as shown in Photo **E**.

Countersink the holes inside the center cabinets.

6. Put the side cabinet back into position and drive the screws though the side of the center cabinet into the face-frame. Also drive screws through the side of the carcase to fasten it to the reveal assembly on the wall. Finally, put shims behind the back of the cabinet if necessary, and fasten the top rear of the cabinet to the studs, as shown in Photo **F**.

Repeat this process for the other side cabinet, then fasten the top center cabinet to the wall. Add the face-frame to the top center cabinet with pocket hole screws.

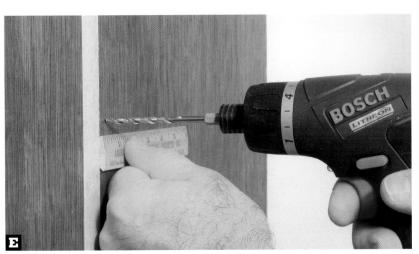

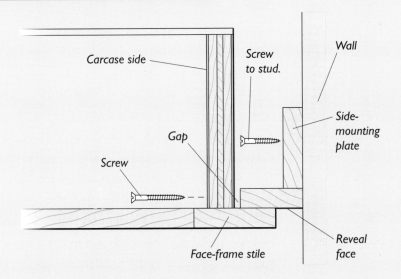

THE REVEAL ASSEMBLY

Carcase side

Screw to stud.

Gap

Screw

Face-frame stile

Wall

Side-mounting plate

Reveal face

Using a reveal assembly at the wall provides a bit of clearance to simplify installation: See the gap in the drawing. A space of about ¼ in. works well if you have no clearance on the other side of the carcase.

The assembly also eliminates tedious scribing of the face-frame to the wall. If any scribing is necessary, do it to the reveal face board before you attach the side mounting plate to it with pocket hole screws.

The gap requires that you go easy on the torque when you drive the screws through the carcase into the reveal assembly. Overdriving will strain the carcase or shift its position.

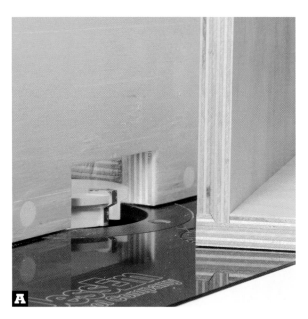

A

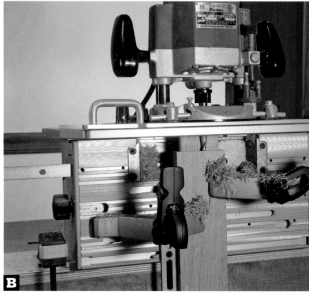

B

Install the Doors, Drawers and Shelves

For a full discussion of the procedures for making doors, drawers, and shelves, please refer to the earlier chapters of the same names.

1. For speed and economy, I made the drawers from 12-mm (½-in.) Baltic birch plywood. A drawer-lock bit in a table-mounted router, as shown in Photo **A**, is a no-nonsense approach to corner joinery. The procedure that begins on p. 103 walks you through the installation of the no-slam slides.

2. The large doors will see regular use, so I used the Leigh FMT jig, shown in Photo **B**, to make snug-fitting mortise and tenon joints.

3. Some of the small doors simply conceal speakers, so they'll be opened only occasionally. For these, I used the matched set of router bits shown in Photo **C**, to make stub tenon joints.

4. After all the doors were out of the clamps, I used a rabbeting bit on their backs so I could slip in the door panels. For the doors with the grill cloth inserts, make a pine frame to simplify the task of stapling the speaker cloth in place, as shown in Photo **D**. Paint the frame black so it won't peek through the fabric. As you stretch and fasten the fabric, make sure to keep the weave squared on the frame.

5. You'll find a thorough discussion of door installation procedures beginning on p. 82, but there is a special detail worth mentioning here. I added Blum's Blumotion to the hinges to ensure that the doors can't slam. Installation is no-tool easy—simply clip the unit to the hinge arm, as shown in Photo **E**.

6. Install standards, then cut the shelves to size. One p. 57, you'll see several ways of concealing raw plywood edges, but here's one more. The router bit set in Photo **F** slices a V-groove in the plywood, and the complementary bit mills the solid edging. After routing, use your

C

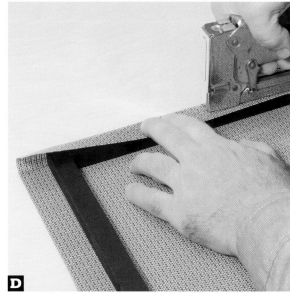

D

E

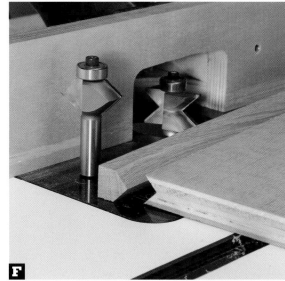

F

TRADE SECRET

Speaker grill cloth is engineered to be acoustically transparent, which means that it has a minimum blocking effect on sound waves traveling through it. Search the Internet and you'll find a wide selection of colors and weaves to suit virtually any decor. You can, though, get decent results from less-expensive materials purchased at a fabric store. A quick test for whether a fabric is suitable is to hold it up to your mouth and blow through it. If you feel any resistance, look for another cloth. Try to be a little discreet with this test, or you'll get plenty of strange looks from the sales staff and other customers.

tablesaw to rip the banding to width. Glue it in place and trim the edges flush.

Installing some period-correct hardware reinforced the Arts and Crafts theme of this project. If you're intimidated about installing the entertainment center's sound and video components, it's easy to get professional help. A skilled installer will be able to optimize your system, coaxing every bit of performance from your gear.

DESIGN
OPTIONS

▲ Full-length cleats behind the main panel anchored solidly to the wall studs allow the flat-screen TV to hang seemingly floating off the surface of the wall.

◄ Making use of every bit of available space, the configuration of the shelves and sides of this entertainment center have been tailored to fit precisely under the stairway in this basement hideaway.

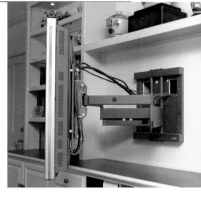

▲ Commercially available mounts will allow you to tailor the angle of the screen to the position of the viewer.

▲ Hinged doors on the side of your entertainment center installation provide a nifty place for convenient access to all your CDs, DVDs and other recorded material.

▲ Sliding panels faced with faux book covers retract to reveal the entertainment center and tucked-away bar. When closed, the wall looks like a complete library.

INSTALLING CABINETS

Buying manufactured cabinets opens the gateway to a wide range of built-in projects throughout your home. For example, you can build a wall of bookcases in the living room or master suite, create a china cabinet in the dining room, or transform a wasted corner into a home office. After you settle on a design, the factory will custom manufacture your cabinets and deliver them, usually within a few weeks.

The laundry room installation on the following pages will introduce you to the procedures you'll use when installing manufactured cabinets for your projects, whether it's a single cabinet or an entire room. You'll witness all the steps, from initial layout to the finishing touches. You'll also discover an innovative method of hanging wall cabinets. It gives you faster and more accurate results and completely eliminates the effort of holding the cabinets in place while you fasten them.

When you see that cabinet installation is a skill you can master, you'll be eager to get going on your own built-ins. ▶ ▶ ▶

Strategies and Tactics

Installing a set of cabinets takes some strategic planning. Installing both base and upper cabinets means two major decisions. First, do you start with the top cabinets or with the bottom? Next, in what sequence do the cabinets go up?

Bottom up or top down?

The old business adage about starting at the bottom and working your way up may not work best as cabinet installation plan. Let's take a brief look at which cabinets to install first.

Bottom-up advocates assert that establishing the horizontal plane of lower cabinets eases the placement of the uppers. After installing the base cabinets, you lay scrap plywood on top, put jacks on that surface, and lift the uppers into position.

Unfortunately, I've often found it extremely difficult to lift cabinets over the base units with-

Glass itself can become a design feature, such as this custom panel with rice paper laminated between clear panes.

out damaging one or the other. And while it's nice to have a level surface on which to lay tools, the installed base cabinets and jacks make it awkward to position shims and drive screws.

In case you haven't already guessed, I much prefer the top-down system. I've found it much easier to lift the cabinets straight up and to have fewer obstructions when fastening them. The one exception is a built-in unit requiring a precise distance between the upper and lower cabinets—an appliance garage, for example. In that case, I'd recommend a bottom-up approach.

Setting the sequence

Even after you've settled the first challenge, you may still wonder which cabinet to set first. Some companies, such as American Woodmark®, eliminate the mystery with a manual that recommends a sequence. If your cabinets don't arrive with that helpful advice—or if you crafted your own—here's a couple of guidelines you can use to figure it out yourself.

• Look for the filler-strip locations. Semi-custom cabinets come in a fixed set of widths (usually in 3-in. increments), with filler strips for the space at the end. Thus, you should usually start at the end opposite the filler. (The exception is when a filler strip merely provides clearance at the wall for opening a door.) The strips also allow you to scribe the cabinet to a wall that's not perfectly straight or plumb. If you build your own face-frame cabinets, provide for scribing with a wide stile at the final end.

• Work away from a corner.
When installing cabinets, it's a good idea not to work yourself into a corner. Install the corner cabinet first and work outward. Setting this big cabinet also gives you a boost of energy from the immediate sense of accomplishment.

Establish the layout lines

In both top-down and bottom-up installations, you'll set layout lines from the bottom up. This procedure will establish the highest floor point within the footprint of your cabinets, and you'll base all your layout lines on that point. The following demonstration uses ordinary levels. You'll find the laser-level procedure on p. 148.

If the room is carpeted, pull the carpet and pad in the cabinet area down to a solid floor surface. Using your overhead view of the cabinet layout, tape the floor to approximate the placement of the base units. The taping doesn't need to be precise, so don't spend too much time on it.

1. Using a level, find the highest spot along each wall within the cabinet area. Put one end of the level at a corner and swing the opposite end in an arc within the cabinet footprint to see whether the floor rises or falls. If the floor falls away from the corner, shim the low end of the level to center the bubble. Then set the corner end of the level on the shims and continue along the wall. If the floor rises away from the

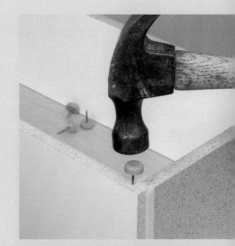

Keep Your Cabinets High and Dry

EVEN A LITTLE BIT OF WATER CAN cause big problems with built-in cabinets. Cabinets sitting in water will wick moisture upward, break down adhesives and delaminate panels. In addition, moisture can set the stage for mold, mildew, and insect invasion.

To help eliminate these problems, install tack glides on the bottom edges of your base cabinets. The glides (usually about ¼ in. thick) will keep the cabinets high and dry unless you have an extremely serious flood. In addition, the space they create will also promote drying. After a flood, pop off the molding at the base to allow air to circulate.

Tack glides are inexpensive flood insurance for base cabinets in moisture-prone areas.

corner, slide your level along the floor, searching for a spot where the floor tilts down.

As you work, you may need several lengths of levels so you can work both parallel and perpendicular to the wall. If your layout runs along two or more walls, put a 1x4 square block at each wall's high point and span between them to discover the highest one (see Photo **A** on p. 160). The blocks let you go over bumps in the floor that aren't important to this process. If your level isn't long enough, put it on top of a straight 2x4.

2. After you've identified the high point, remove any blocks and use a level to transfer the high point to the nearest wall. Make the mark at the bottom of the level, as shown in Photo **B** on p. 160. Measure the actual height of your base cabinets, and add the thickness of a tack glide if you'll be using them to protect your cabinets from water (see "Keep Your Cabinets High and Dry" on p. 159.)

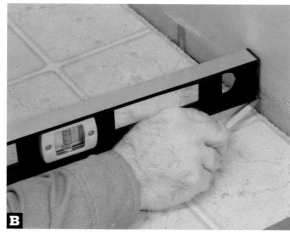

As soon as you receive your shipment of cabinets, open each box and inspect the contents for freight damage and manufacturing defects. If you don't discover a damaged cabinet until later, it could bring the installation to a screeching halt. After inspection, repack the cabinets to prevent damage.

Organize the Cabinets

WHENEVER POSSIBLE, I LIKE TO store the cabinets in a staging area and move each one to the installation site as it's needed. Keep the cabinets inside their shipping boxes as long as possible.

Remove the doors and shelves from each cabinet before you move them. Numbering the doors and cabinets, makes it easy to re-unite the components. You'll be tempted to lean them against a wall, but it's safer to store them flat. Separate them with sheets of cardboard sliced from the shipping boxes.

3. Using a long level, as shown in Photo **C**, draw a horizontal line indicating the top of the base cabinets.

Go back to the highest floor-point mark you made earlier, and measure to the top of the wall cabinets. The American Woodmark installation guide for these cabinets specified a height of 90 in. AFF (above finished floor). This mark verifies vertical clearance for cabinets against a soffit. Next, measure the actual height of your upper cabinets, and draw a level line at their lower edge. Drawing both upper and lower lines may seem redundant, but it helps eliminate errors, especially if you're installing cabinets of various heights.

4. Using a stud finder, as shown in Photo **D**, mark the center of each stud at three locations: just above the top line of the base cabinets, below the lower line of the wall cabinets, and above the line at the top of the cabinets.

Installing Wall Cabinets

Wall cabinet installation traditionally relies on a ledger screwed to the wall to support the lower back edge. We'll take a quick look at that method, but then you'll discover a more dependable system that gives better results faster.

Hanging wall cabinets: The old way

The old way of installing wall cabinets begins by screwing a 2x2 ledger strip to the wall, with its top edge on the line of the bottom of the cabinets. After transferring the stud marks to the front of the 2x2, you lift the cabinet into place. A brawny and patient helper can support the cabinet while you plumb and fasten it.

A somewhat better solution adds a temporary brace—a 2x4 about ¾-in. longer than the floor-to-cabinet-bottom distance—to keep the cabinets propped up on the ledger. A carpet scrap at the top prevents scratches. Even with this brace, it's a good idea to have a helper stabilize the setup. Accidentally kicking out the brace won't be any good for you or the cabinets.

Install wall cabinets: A new approach

I was never fond of a 2x4 supporting a cabinet. It's not particularly secure if you're working alone, and kicking at a stick never seemed like an accurate way of fine-tuning a cabinet's fit. And while a 2x2 does a good job supporting the back of a cabinet, it blocks you from inserting shims.

If the top of the wall leans forward, you can screw only the top of the cabinet. You then need to remove the ledger and shim out the bottom before screwing it into place. But when you pull the bottom out from the wall, you strain the cabinet because it's already fastened on top.

To solve these problems, I wanted a method that would support the cabinet but still let me shim it at each stud. I call the solution the "Slingshot System," taking its name from the shape of the brace shown on p. 162. You just screw a brace at each stud even with the layout line. When the stud is too close to a corner for a full brace, use a left- or right-hand half-brace.

The other component of the system is a step box that also serves as the base for a steel jack post. This type of post is usually used to lift a sagging floor, so it has far more strength than you'll ever need. The one I bought costs about the same at two take-out pizzas, and adjusts from 2 ft. 10 in. to 4 ft. 7 in. At full extension, it will hold 7 tons, 9 tons when shortened.

Construct the braces and step box as shown in "The Slingshot System for Hanging Cabinets" p. 162, and begin by prepping the units.

Prep the cabinets

To prep manufactured cabinets, first cut and apply the manufacturer's prefinished panel or "skin" to the side of any cabinet that will be exposed.

1. Once you've cut the panel, lay a ¼-in. bead of construction adhesive (I use the type formulated for panels) around the perimeter of the cabinet's side. Keep the bead about 1 in. from the edges so you don't get any messy squeeze-out. Run a couple of zigzag beads on the middle of the side, then lower the skin in place, as

PRO TIP

Before you begin a cabinet installation, remove and store any interior doors to the room. This eliminates an obstruction that can cause or receive damage.

TRADE SECRET

After positioning the skin, gently tap it down and then pull it upward to create long strings of adhesive. Wait a few seconds, then put the skin back in place. This procedure helps promote a quicker initial grip plus a stronger ultimate bond.

The Slingshot System for Hanging Cabinets

INVEST A BIT OF TIME TO MAKE THE components of the Slingshot System and you'll earn big dividends in improved accuracy while also saving time and effort.

Use the dimensioned drawing below left to make a set of wall braces. Even for large installations, you'll probably never need more than four full braces plus a right- and left-hand half-brace.

Following the steps illustrated, construct the step box for the jack using the dimensions shown in the drawing below right. Be sure to have the column on hand before you make the box in case you need to customize any of the dimensions. If your project involves a long run, consider making a pair of step boxes and using two jacks.

1. Rip and crosscut all the parts to size and assemble the sides and ends with glue and finishing nails or screws. Cut the top and mark the position of the hand hole. Drill a 1-in. hole at each end, then jigsaw the edges of the holes.

Routing a ¼-in. roundover on both sides of the slot eliminates sharp edges and makes it more user-friendly. Fasten the top to the base assembly, as shown in Photo **A**.

2. Mark the position of the post hole, and drill it with a hole saw, as shown in Photo **B**. Round off the top rim of this hole, if desired. Make sure the plug fits inside your column.

3. Set the brace directly under the top, and mark through the centered plug, as shown in Photo **C**. Screw and glue the plug to the brace, then fasten the brace inside the box at the bottom, as indicated in Photo **D**

4. Insert the column through the hole, and engage its end over the plug to anchor it securely. Adjust the column's height for your project. If the two parts of the post don't fit

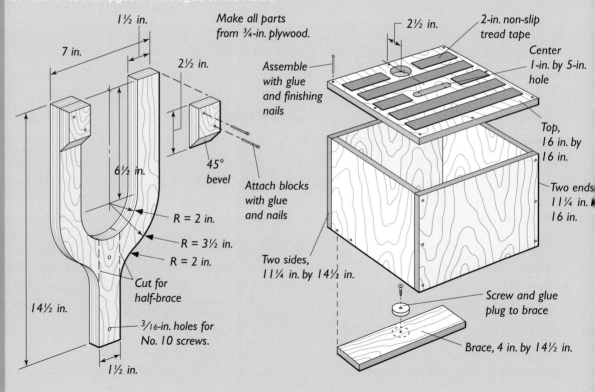

Make all parts from ¾-in. plywood.

1½ in.

7 in.

2½ in.

6½ in.

45° bevel

R = 2 in.

R = 3½ in.

R = 2 in.

Cut for half-brace

14½ in.

³⁄₁₆-in. holes for No. 10 screws.

1½ in.

Assemble with glue and finishing nails

Attach blocks with glue and nails

2½ in.

2-in. non-slip tread tape

Center 1-in. by 5-in. hole

Top, 16 in. by 16 in.

Two ends 11¼ in. 16 in.

Two sides, 11¼ in. by 14½ in.

Screw and glue plug to brace

Brace, 4 in. by 14½ in.

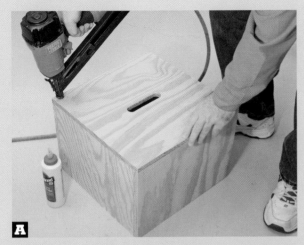

A

B

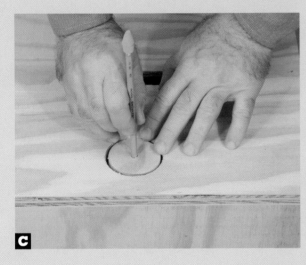

C

D

snugly, tighten the fit by tapping in some tapered softwood shims, as shown in Photo **E**.

After cleaning the packing grease off the circular metal plate, I epoxied it to the top of the column. To create a lift platform atop the threaded rod, I drilled a $\frac{7}{8}$-in. hole $\frac{7}{8}$-in. deep into a $1\frac{1}{2}$-in. by $2\frac{3}{4}$-in. 5-in. oak block. With double-faced tape, I adhered a $\frac{1}{16}$-in.-thick sheet of plumbing gasket material to the top of the block to create a surface that resists slipping and scratching. Your column may have a different screw mechanism setup. If so, you can easily adapt the directions.

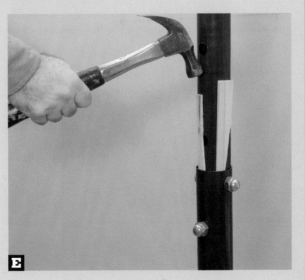

E

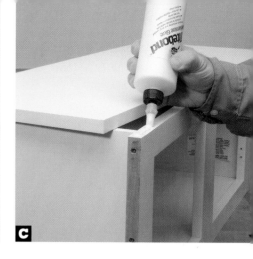

A

B

C

Join and Conquer

SOMETIMES IT'S A GOOD idea to join two or more cabinets together before installing them. To do this on face-frame cabinets, align and screw the stiles together, adding blocking between the units near the back edge, if necessary, to square them.

With frameless cabinets, you can skip the blocking and simply join the cabinet sides with connector bolts (see p. 127).

No matter which type of cabinets you're uniting, it's essential to assemble them on a flat surface. I've found that a hollow-core door set on sawhorses makes a dependably flat surface that's easy to move to the job site.

Don't get too ambitious linking multiple cabinets together—you can quickly create an assembly that's too heavy or bulky to lift comfortably.

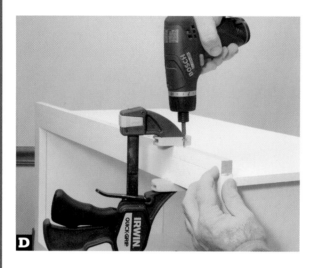

D

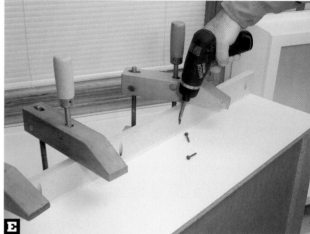

E

shown in Photo **A**. Some people shoot a few finishing nails to make the installation instant, but I prefer clamping because it eliminate unsightly nail holes.

2. Smooth the skin with your hands to ensure it's flat and properly aligned. Top the skin with plywood to distribute the pressure and pile on some weight, as shown in Photo **B**. Clamping the ends ensures a close bond.

3. There's another procedure that's similar to skinning that you may occasionally need when the bottom of a cabinet is above eye level. In this laundry room, that occurred for the high horizontal cabinet above the washer and dryer. In a similar situation, you would first add any filler strips to the front stiles, then cut a panel to make a smooth surface at the bottom of the cabinet. I fastened the melamine-clad panel

with glue, as shown in Photo **C**, plus a few air-driven finishing nails.

4. Filler-strip installation is another important prep procedure. The cabinet layout plans will specify sizes, but you need to double-check these against actual measurements at the installation site. Rip filler strips to width and cut them to length. When you screw a strip in place, carefully align its face with the cabinet stile, as shown in Photo **D**. I stay away from glue and nails for this step in case I need to remove the strip to change its size.

5. If the filler strip is too wide to easily permit drilling through its edge, substitute pocket-hole screws, as shown in Photo **E**.

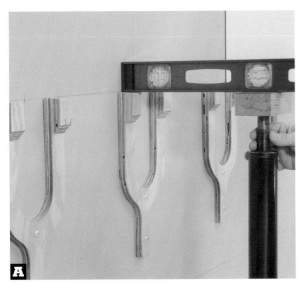

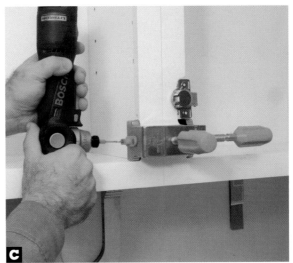

Hang the wall cabinets

Screw a line of slingshot braces along the wall, aligning their top edge with the bottom layout line. Put the jack column in the step box, positioning the screw so that it will be directly under the lower rail of the cabinet and centered side-to-side along the cabinet's width.

1. Span a level between the slingshot brace and the lift platform, as shown in Photo **A**, and adjust the screw to center the bubble.

2. Cut a straight piece of lumber to the height of your cabinet, and check at each stud to see whether the wall tilts forward, back, or is actually plumb. This step, shown in Photo **B**, forewarns you whether the top or bottom of the cabinet requires shimming. You can even place your shims now, taping them to the wall so that they don't fall. Set the cabinet on the slingshot braces and the screw jack.

3. Align the front edges of a pair of cabinets and clamp them together. Cabinet Claw clamps

from Jorgensen® are a real time saver because they hold the cabinets firmly side-to-side but also have a padded clamp at the front to persuade the face-frame edges into perfect alignment.

As shown in Photo **C**, use the bushing in the side of the clamp as a guide to drill a pilot hole through the first frame and into the target one.

4. Swing the bushing holder out of the way to reveal the access hole that enables you to drive the screw joining the stiles, as shown

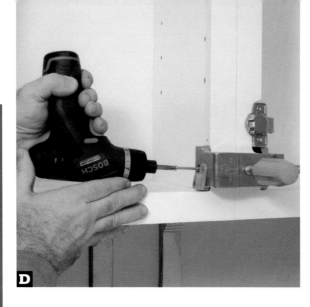

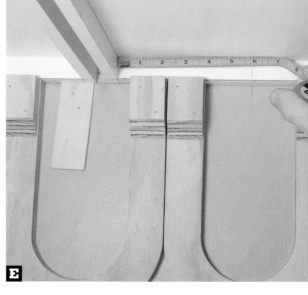

PRO TIP

If your built-in job involves jumbo cabinets, make sure you'll be able to maneuver them into the room. If necessary, cut a full-size cardboard template of the top view of the cabinets. Hold the template level to verify that your doorway provides enough clearance.

in Photo **D**. I'll usually drive three screws through each stile, with the middle one installed from the opposite direction.

5. At the bottom of the cabinet, measure from the side of the cabinet to the centerline of each stud, as shown in Photo **E**, and transfer the location to the inside top of the cabinet. Adjust the shims, if necessary, to bring the front plane of the cabinet plumb. Drill a pilot hole, and

drive a cabinet screw through the shims and into the stud, as shown in Photo **F**.

6. Fasten the bottom of the cabinet by driving a cabinet screw through the shims and into the stud, as shown in Photo **G**.

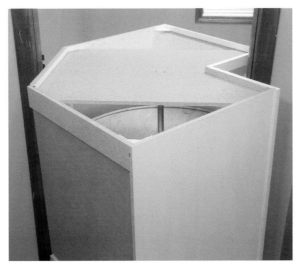

In some cases, getting into the installation room can be a snug situation. Here's a base corner unit that just fit into the laundry room.

Installing Base Cabinets

I like to use a padded four-wheel furniture dolly to move cabinets into the installation area. Using one conserves your energy, plus you're much less likely to damage the cabinets.

If you accounted for tack glides when you planned the layout (see p. 159), tap them into the bottom edge of the cabinet now.

1. Position the base cabinet against the wall to see whether you need to install shims along its rear edge. If so, stack shims at the top of the back to gauge the height required, as shown in Photo **A**. Slide the cabinet forward, place the shims on the floor, and lift the cabinet onto them.

2. Level the front of the cabinet by placing shims, as shown in Photo **B**. A short pry bar enables you to easily lift the cabinet to insert the shims.

Align the front stiles of neighboring base cabinets with the same Cabinet Claw procedure you used for the upper cabinets.

Cutting Custom Shims

I CUT SHIMS FROM SCRAP to a uniform 1½ in. by 8-in., about the same size as commercial softwood shims. I also chop some of them into squares to raise the front of base units.

To make it easy to quickly grab the thickness you need, make each thickness from a distinct material. For this project, my bucket had shims from ½-in. plywood, ¼-in. hardboard, ⅛-in. plywood and 1-mm self-stick vinyl floor tiles. I get the cheapest tiles at the home center and use a paper cutter to slice the 12-in. squares into 1½-in. by 6-in. strips. You can also cut these tiles with a utility knife.

There are two ways to create a toekick platform: attach it to the cabinet, as shown here, or fasten a platform to the floor. The entertainment center project (see p. 142) and closet cubes (see p. 172) utilize the second solution. Choosing which approach to select sometimes requires a bit of thought.

In this case, the homeowners said they planned to install a ceramic tile floor in the laundry room within the next three years, and wanted the base cabinets removed at that time. Fastening a platform to the floor would have complicated both removal and reinstallation, so attaching it to the cabinet became the logical choice.

3. Make sure that the gap between the cabinet sides remains uniform front to back. Clamp shims between the cabinets, as shown in Photo **C**, to maintain the spacing while you attach the cabinet to the wall.

4. Use connector bolts or Chicago bolts to unite two cabinets whose construction does not permit conventional joining of the face-frame stiles. An example is the angled cabinet shown in Photo **D**.

5. Joining base cabinets with connector bolts can be useful for another reason. Sometimes you need to carefully align the edge of base and upper cabinets, as shown in Photo **E**. In

this case, a 90-in. tall pantry goes to the left, so establishing a plumb line was critical. I simply backed out a couple of cabinet screws, persuaded the unitized base assembly into position, and drove the screws again.

6. The pantry is only 6 in. deep, so I joined it to its deeper neighbors with the technique shown in Photo **F**. First, drill a pilot hole through the stile of the shallower cabinet and the side of the deeper one. Then, drive the screw from the opposite direction to unite the cabinets.

7. Don't overlook adapting a cabinet for a special function. Photo **G** shows the bottom of a wall cabinet transformed into a window seat.

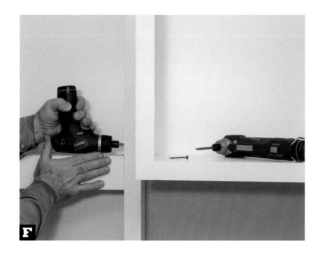

F

G

as seen in Photo **A**. Doing this work in the shop ensured the assemblies were flat and square, simplifying installation. Glue and air-driven finish nails hold the moldings in place.

2. Use an offset dovetail saw, as shown in Photo **B**, to slice away the excess length of shims. Save these offcuts for your next project. Remove the screws holding the slingshot braces. If a backsplash won't cover the holes, patch them and touch up the paint.

3. Careful caulking will eliminate distracting shadow lines to make your installation job look

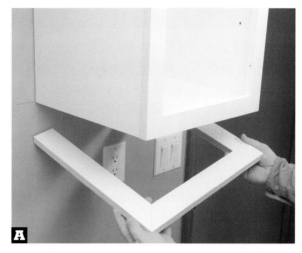

A

The model, usually made 24 in. deep for use above a refrigerator was special-ordered 18 in. deep. I added filler strips to both front stiles, blocked out the sides for new ends with toekick notches, and completed the design with a pine toekick.

Finishing touches

From an aesthetic standpoint, a molding along the bottom of the upper cabinets adds a shadow line or a decorative detail. From a practical approach, it also helps hide undercabinet lights.

1. For this installation, the design specified a square-edged molding made from filler-strip stock. I mitered the corners and joined them with biscuits to create L- and U-shaped units,

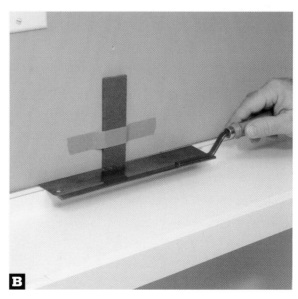

B

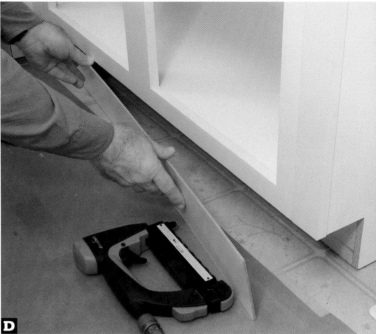

WHAT CAN GO WRONG

Never drill the mounting holes for handles or knobs until after you've installed the doors. The risk of error is simply too great, and concealing a botched hole position is a real challenge.

seamless. To get a crisp line along painted walls, run a strip of masking tape even with the cabinet side before caulking, as shown in Photo **C**. Dampen your finger with water, and slide it along the caulk to remove the excess and leave a smooth surface. Peel away the tape, and move to the next seam.

4. You'll use prefinished "skin" stock to cover the raw fronts of the toekick areas, as shown in Photo **D**. Measure for a close fit along the floor or even scribe to fit if you're finicky. In most cases, I'll install a base shoe molding at the floor line so there's no need to get obsessive about the fit of these skins. Apply construction adhesive to the skin, and then drive a few headless pins to hold it in place until the bond's complete. I drive the pins up high where they can't be seen, and down low where the base shoe will conceal the holes.

5. Install and adjust the doors. Hinge adjustment systems vary, so you'll need to learn how to move the doors so that they're level and aligned. The hinge shown in Photo **E**, for example, has a slot that enables you to move the door up and down. The screw engaged by the driver in the photo moves the door left and right over the opening.

6. You'll sometimes run into tight-clearance situations where you need just a bit more room for a door to swing. One quick solution for the hinge type shown in Photo **F** involves washers as shims to shift the door. Insert the washers between the hinge baseplate and the edge of the stile. Switching to a slightly longer screw ensures that you don't compromise holding power. For other hinge types, you may need to install a shim strip along the inner edge of the cabinet stile.

E

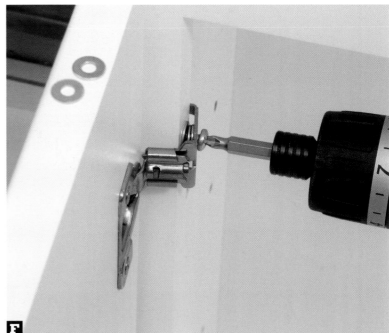

F

7. I made the drilling jig shown in Photo **G** to ensure deadly accuracy when drilling the installation holes for the knobs. The registration blocks on the jig's edges ensure proper positioning for every possible knob location. I drilled a ⅝-in. hole at the knob's centerpoint and tapped in an insert with a ridged outer perimeter that grips the wood. The threads inside the insert enable you to screw in a hardened steel bushing that matches the diameter of the hole you're drilling. In this case, I chose a ³⁄₁₆-in. bushing for the No. 8 machine screws furnished with the knobs. (Lee Valley is one source for the inserts and bushings.) When you need to reverse the jig, remove the bushing and screw it in from the other side. A backer board prevents tearout where the bit exits the door, and it's held by the clamp that secures the jig. A masking tape flag on the bit lets you know when you've drilled far enough.

G

CLOSET ORGANIZATION

Many residential closets resemble black holes, the cosmic feature that sucks in surrounding matter so powerfully that not even light can escape. If your closet is dark and doesn't let you retrieve items easily, it's time for a makeover.

You can choose from several systems that use modular "off the shelf" components to customize the space for the items you want to organize. In the master bedroom, for example, you'll want to create an attractive but efficient area where you can prepare for a day of work or begin to unwind for a restful evening. In a guest bedroom, you may want to install a drawer unit so visitors don't need to live out of a suitcase. And a cramped closet with architectural challenges could become an efficient home for out-of-season clothing.

Closet renovations add value and convenience to your home, but perhaps the biggest reward is the warm satisfaction of transforming chaos into order—at least in your small part of the universe. ▶ ▶ ▶

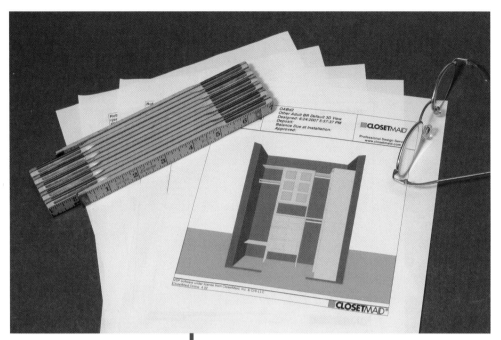

Planning the Installation

When you're standing in the closet-materials aisle at a home center, it's tough to visualize how the components will go together in an installation you'll like. It's like going to the auto parts store and ordering all the pieces to build a car.

Fortunately, at least one company has taken the uncertainty out of closet planning. Visit the ClosetMaid® website (www.closetmaid.com) for professional design options. Enter the dimensions of your closet and answer some questions about your storage needs. For a fee equivalent to a fast-food meal, you'll get two design options in about four days. If you don't like them, you can even receive one alteration at no charge. The service includes a perspective view, a plan (overhead) view, elevations, and a list of the components.

If you want to plan your own design, see p. 12 for standard closet dimensions. You'll find the data especially helpful if you're planning a closet for a growing child or a person with physical limitations.

Storage Cubes: A Versatile Problem Solver

The awkward dimensions of another closet presented a challenge. Worse, the ceiling followed the roofline, ending at a 2-ft. kneewall at the far end. The builder had installed rods on both sides, but that left no center access. The homeowner abandoned the rods and crammed the space with cardboard boxes for out-of-season clothes. But the design also included shoe racks on the side walls, so retrieving anything often involved unloading the entire closet.

The stacked boxes provided a clue to the design solution: cubicles hugging each side wall, stepping down to follow the ceiling slope. Home centers sell very affordable melamine-clad cubes about 12 in. high, wide, and deep. Each side of the closet required two 9-cube (3 by 3) units and one 6-cube (2 by 3) unit. At the far end of the closet, one cube was trimmed from a 9-cube unit to accommodate the ceiling slope.

Each wall now boasts 23 cubic feet—more than most full-size refrigerator/freezer combos—plus 6 sq. ft. of countertop surface on each side.

Setting the storage cubes

Demolition was the first step. After minor repairs and a fresh coat of paint on the walls and ceiling, the space was ready.

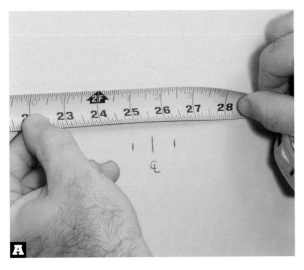

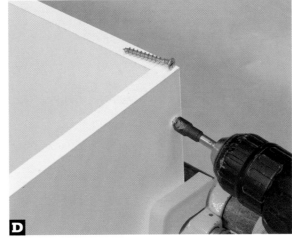

1. On a wall you will eventually cover with cabinets, locate and mark the edges of each stud with a stud finder. Mark the centerline, as shown in Photo **A**. Record the location of the studs along each wall.

2. Build a ladder-shaped toekick base for the cabinets from 4-in. wide stock. I used white melamine for the front so I could eliminate sanding, priming, and painting. Driving pocket hole screws, as shown in Photo **B**, eliminated any visible fastener holes.

3. Shim the base level along each dimension, as shown in Photo **C**. Secure the base to the studs

and to the floor. Use pocket hole screws to fasten the cross braces to the floor.

4. A half-sheet of plywood makes a flat assembly surface for the cubes. I flushed up the ends and edges of the first corner with pipe clamps, but when I drove the first screws, their heads didn't pull flush with the surface. That would create problems when joining the cubes, but torquing the screws more would spin the MDF into a powder with no holding strength. So I countersunk the holes to create a shallow recess, as shown in Photo **D**. Driving the screws flush pulled the joint together snugly.

Magnetic Screw Bowl

A MAGNETIC MECHANIC'S BOWL (AVAILABLE AT AUTO-PARTS stores) keeps steel fasteners from scattering, even if you accidentally kick the container.

WHAT CAN GO WRONG

Before you start setting cabinets on a toekick base, make sure you haven't left any tools behind. Entombing a tool is embarrassing and expensive.

5. Insert two short dowels into the vertical dividers and secure each divider with a screw through the top. Align a horizontal divider so you can insert long dowels through it and into the vertical dividers. As shown in Photo **E**, a deadblow mallet gently persuades the parts into alignment.

6. Add another side of short vertical dividers and a long horizontal divider. At this point, you may find it more convenient to rotate the assembly vertically, as shown in Photo **F**. Be careful, though, because the assembly is still shaky at this time. Complete the cube unit by

clamping and driving the assembly screws.

7. Make sure all joints are tight, then check for square by measuring for equal diagonals. As shown in Photo **G**, drive the nails square to the surface so the tips don't penetrate the inside edges. Space the nails no farther than 6 in. apart.

8. Set the first cabinet in place. Insert shims, if needed, and then drill pilot holes through the back and into the studs. (For more about shims, see p. 167.) Driving cabinet hanging screws at both the top and bottom of the cube unit, as shown in Photo **H**, firmly anchors the assembly.

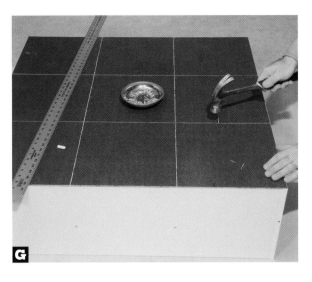

G

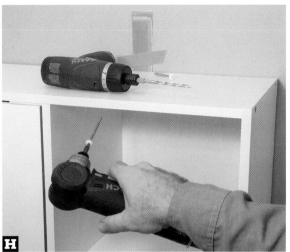

H

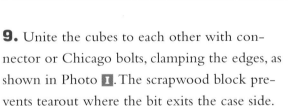

I

J

9. Unite the cubes to each other with connector or Chicago bolts, clamping the edges, as shown in Photo **I**. The scrapwood block prevents tearout where the bit exits the case side.

10. The doors provided for inexpensive concealed storage, as shown in Photo **J**, come with plastic hinges that are far from furniture-grade, but appropriate for a closet.

11. You can use the push-in plastic screw covers supplied by the manufacturer, but I've found they sometimes eject themselves. In addition, you can't use them at all if the screw is driven

Strengthen Your Back

THE MANUFACTURER PROVIDED five folded paperboard squares for the back for the unit. This solution makes sense from a packaging standpoint, but not from an aesthetic or structural viewpoint. So I bought ⅛-in. hardboard with a white finish—the kind used for dry-erase marker boards.
It's smooth and durable, but best of all, it didn't require me to crack open a can of paint. I cut the panel about ⅛-in undersize overall so the edges wouldn't be in the way when joining the cubes.

PRO TIP

Pencil lines are tough to see on dark surfaces such as hardboard. Instead, mark with ordinary white chalk for a bright stroke.

WHAT CAN GO WRONG

Irregularities in the wall, especially if it tips forward at the top, could prevent you from aligning the edges of neighboring cubes. Test-fit the units by temporarily stacking and clamping them in position. Shift the assembly until you're satisfied with the location. Then unclamp and remove the top cabinets, being careful not to shift the lower ones. Now you can fasten them in place with confidence.

PROTIP

Partially drive two nails into the studs along your level installation line. These will support the metal while you fasten it.

too deeply. I prefer concealing the screws with self-adhesive dots, as shown in Photo **K**. (McFeely's, http://www.mcfeelys.com, carries these dots in a wide spectrum of colors and woodgrains.)

12. The completed installation, shown in Photo **L**, demonstrates how a catchall area became an efficient closet—eye-catching and accessible. Fabric drawers brighten the installation and make rearrangements nearly effortless.

Hang-Track Closet System

A hang-track system will put you on the fast track to completing your closet. Its key component is the horizontal track set near the top of the walls. Screwing it to the studs gives it a firm structural connection and ensures that all of the other components will be level. This system side-steps concerns about uneven floors and the hassle of dealing with baseboards.

Hang-track is usually teamed with wire shelving, and you'll find plenty of other accessories, including closet rods made to sweep uninterrupted around corners. Most of the parts snap together or require nothing more sophisticated than a screwdriver. Simple installation techniques and modular components make it easy to alter configurations if your storage needs change. You'll also find cabinets for a hang track, allowing you to further tailor the system to your needs.

Install a hang track

To install a hang track, draw a level line for its bottom edge at the desired height (84 in. is common in a closet with an 8-ft. ceiling). Find and mark the location of each stud with electronic stud sensor. Most hang tracks feature mounting holes at 8-in. intervals, fitting studs on either 16-in. or 24-in. centers. Match these holes to the studs—otherwise you'd need to drill through the metal of the track.

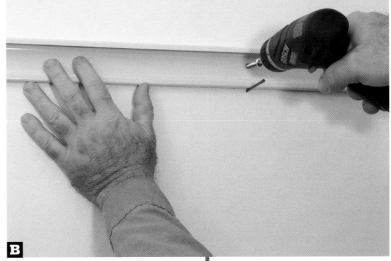

WHAT CAN GO WRONG

If you must cut a hanging standard to length, be sure you cut the bottom end. Cutting at the top of the standard would remove the notches that grip the hanging track.

PRO TIP

There are two strategies for dealing with baseboard molding. You can either notch the back of the cabinet to create clearance or remove the molding, trimming and reinstalling it to fit around the cabinet.

1. Measure from a corner of the closet to the center of the first stud, then transfer this dimension from the centerpoint of a hole toward the end of the track, as shown in Photo A. I prefer marking the back of the track, which has a wide smooth surface. Hacksawing the track at the mark will then center a mounting hole at each stud. Cut the other end of the track to fit the length of the wall.

2. Using the mounting holes in the track as guides, drill ⁹⁄₆₄-in. pilot holes into the studs, and drive No. 12 sheet-metal screws that are at least 2 in. long, as shown in Photo B. The hang track must bear the entire weight of your

shelving system, so don't rely on hollow-wall drywall anchors. If you're working in masonry, use anchors and screws.

3. Snap the standards into the track, as shown in Photo C, then space them no further than 24 in. on center nor further than 4 in. from the end of a shelf. It isn't necessary to place them at a stud location.

4. Using a level, check each standard for plumb, then mark the location of each mounting screw with a scratch awl, as shown in Photo D. Drywall anchors and screws are adequate for this step because their role is not weight-bearing. The screw merely keeps the standard from

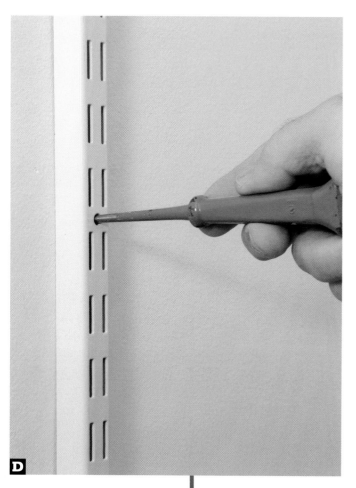

D

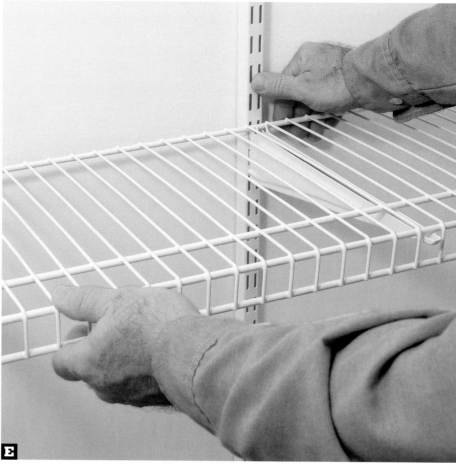

E

TRADE SECRET

The base unit of an RTA cabinet usually sits directly on the floor. But since perfectly flat and level floors are virtually non-existent, the unit includes leveling feet that screw into the bottom of the side panels, simplifying installation.

shifting sideways, so one fastener centered in the length of each standard will do.

5. Lock the shelf brackets into the standards at the desired height, and then snap the shelving into place, as shown in Photo **E**. Use bolt cutters or a hacksaw to trim the shelves to length. Hanging-rod supports and other accessories simply snap onto the shelving.

Custom Closet Storage Unit

Ready-to-assemble (RTA) cabinets are at the top end of the closet-system hierarchy. With them, you can create an installation that's much more than open shelving and hanging rods. You can add doors with glass, drawers in a variety of depths, corner units—even cubbyholes for shoes.

1. Assemble the base units with the supplied screws, and snap in the screw cover caps on sides that will be exposed, as shown in Photo **A**, on p. 182. Be careful you don't drive the screws too deeply, or the caps won't grip the drive recess. In the photo, you'll notice dowels inserted into holes in the top end of the sides, enabling you to stack the units. If you don't use the dowels, you can fill the hole with a plastic plug (visible near the chuck of the drill).

2. Put the base cabinet in position, and stack the upper cabinet, if you're installing one. Shim the edge against the wall to adjust for plumb.

Installing RTA Cabinets Over Carpet

READY-TO-ASSEMBLE CABINETS are made to order for installing on a smooth flooring surface. But setting a unit on carpeting isn't a great idea. The weight of the unit and its contents will sink into the soft surface over time, ruining the initial level of your installation. Besides, to change the floor covering in the future, you would need to uninstall the closet system. I thought about trimming away the carpet and pad so that the cabinet would rest on the floor, but working with carpet isn't one of my strong suits.

The solution I settled on is a wall-mounted elevated platform. This eliminated any settlement issues and also bypassed the necessity of dealing with the base-board. I chose 2x3 lumber (measuring 1½-in. by 2½-in.) and anchored the ledger boards to the studs with 3½-in. deck screws.

Pocket hole screws made it fast and easy to add the other components. I faced the platform's front edge with strips ripped from an extra shelf, attaching them with construction adhesive and a few screws. Including the face strip, the platform's depth equals the width of the cabinet's sides. I mounted the top of the platform 10 in. above the floor to compensate for the amount I shortened the sides of the base units in the next step.

After marking the position of the shelf's lower edge onto the inner face of the side, I disassembled the cabinet and sawed off the "leg" projection, as shown at right. Using a zero-clearance tablesaw insert and a blade designed for laminate minimizes chipout. I gave the same shortening treatment to the storage tower on the adjacent wall.

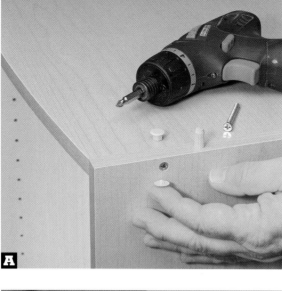

A

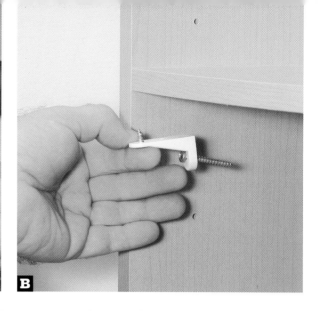

B

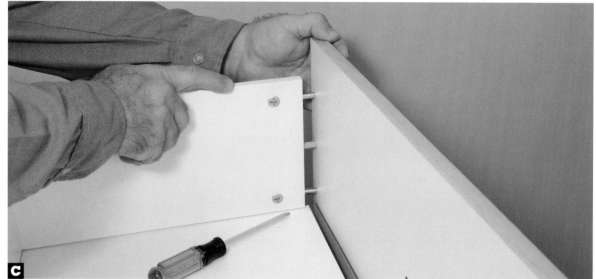

C

PRO TIP

The manufacturer of the cabinets shown in this installation doesn't supply backs. While backless can be appealing for a lady's evening dress, it's not desirable for cabinets. Even a thin back will give a big boost to the strength and stability of a cabinet. Choose prefinished hardboard as shown on p. 177, regular hardboard, or plywood.

PRO TIP

The right and left of drawer slides is determined by your viewpoint when facing the front of the drawer and carcase.

If you installed backs in your cabinets, you can drill pilot holes and drive screws into the studs. Otherwise, use the plastic angles furnished with the cabinet, as shown in Photo **B**. Use a short screw to fasten the angle to the cabinet, and drive a long screw into the stud.

3. If your storage unit includes drawers, you'll discover that their construction is very easy. As you can see in Photo **C**, dowels align the parts, and twisting a screwdriver in the knock-down fasteners draws the joints tightly together.

4. Fasten the drawer slides to the bottom of the drawers and to the inside of the cabinet carcase. You'll usually find the orientation of the drawer slide members identified with an R or L stamped into the metal. In this case, though, I discovered the letter "L" on the axle of the nylon roller, as shown in Photo **D**.

5. This cabinet included glass doors, and installing the glazing with the supplied clips and screws was very simple. Installing the hinges, as shown in Photo **E**, was also very easy. See p. 83 for more information on adjusting Euro hinges to achieve a perfect door fit. Complete the hardware installation by adding the closet rods.

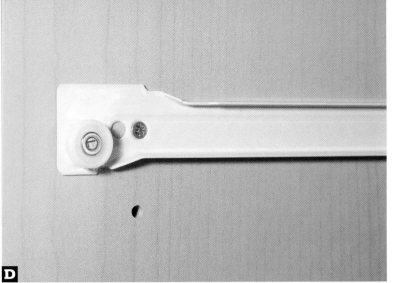

6. The manufacturer's plan for this closet showed the top shelves spanning from the sides of the cabinets to the walls. But this required additional hardware and a lot of fussy fitting. Instead, I merely slapped shelf boards on top of the units for an uninterrupted surface. For support along the wall edges, I installed 3½-in.-wide edge-banded white melamine strips. Where the shelf changes direction, I reinforced the top of the joint with ½-in. round-head sheet metal screws driven through steel mending plates, as shown in Photo **F**. I usually install these plates while the shelf boards are in position atop the cabinets, but photographing it at floor level was more practical.

7. The detail photo of the completed installation, Photo **G**, (shows how the elevated platform seems to levitate the cabinets above the floor for a light and spacious feeling.

WHAT CAN GO WRONG

Be careful
when installing clips that hold glass in place. Apply too much torque, and you'll snap the glass. I prefer using a manual screwdriver for this process because it's much more controlled than a drill/driver. Snug the clip just to the point where it makes contact with the glass without rattling.

INDEX